CUENTOS
PANAMEÑOS

To David and Emily—

May these words of
hope be your
words too.

R.A.B.

CUENTOS PANAMEÑOS

Stories
of Struggle and Hope
in Rural Panama

RICHARD ALLEN BOWER

ILLUSTRATED BY STEPHANIE BOWER

Friendship Press • New York

Some of these stories originally appeared in *Anglican and Episcopal History/The Historical Magazine of the Protestant Episcopal Church* 61, nos. 2, 3. They are reprinted here with permission.

Editorial Offices:
475 Riverside Drive, New York, NY 10115

Distribution Offices:
P.O. Box 37844, Cincinnati, OH 45222-0844

Manufactured in the United States of America

Library of Congress Cataloging-in-Publication Data

Bower, Richard Allen.
    Cuentos panameños : stories of struggle and hope in rural Panama / Richard Allen Bower.
      p. cm.
    ISBN 0-377-00249-6
    1. Panamanian literature—Panama—Monte Claro. 2. Panamanian literature—20th century. 3. Monte Claro (Panama)—Social life and customs—Literary collections. I. Title.
PQ7528.5.M652B68 1993
863—dc20   92-20850
                                           CIP

For Stephanie,
compañera

Contents

7

Acknowledgments

A book is always a community affair. I thank those scattered friends of my community who encouraged me in this effort. Most of all I thank James Ottley, Bishop of the Episcopal Church of Panama, who invited me to work in his country; Elizabeth Barahona, who taught me most of what I know about rural life in Central America; the people of Monte Claro, who let me tell their story; the Episcopal Divinity School in Cambridge, Massachusetts, which through a Procter Fellowship gave me time and space to work; Donald Winslow at EDS, who accompanied me in my writing with wise and honest advice; and Jean Smith and Louise Kingston, who read my work with care and were gentle but right in their suggestions.

Introduction

THIRTY minutes by car from Panama City, west on the Panamerican Highway, one comes to a small town made up of several *barrios* located on both sides of the highway. Arraiján is its name. Clusters of cinder-block houses, most of them stuccoed and brightly painted, make up this village, a community surrounded on all sides by foothills leading west to the more mountainous interior of the country.

In spite of the development of this area near to Panama City, tropical vegetation still abounds. Arraiján is filled with palm trees and *plátanos,* almond and banana, mango and other less common varieties of tropical fruit-bearing trees. On the flat low-lying areas near the town are spread the ever-present pampas grasses.

Most of the people of Arraiján make their living in Panama City, commuting on the brightly painted buses that leave hourly from Arraiján. The people live simply, without a lot of money: day laborers, most of them, with a scattering among them of government employees or small shop owners.

Beyond Arraiján, and into the mountains that dip down to the ocean about ten kilometers away to the southwest, are scattered a number of smaller settlements, or *aldeas.* With lovely names like Cerro Silvestre Barrunga, Lomas del Río and San Antonio, these villages — or better, clusters of houses — depend on Arraiján and on the City for services such as transportation, hospitals, jobs, roads, and education.

Each of these smaller communities has its own organization — a town council, perhaps, or a committee for local work projects. Many of the folk who live in these villages are related by blood or marriage. At times some of the smaller communities seem like great extended families, so filled are they with brothers and sisters, aunts and uncles, cousins, and grandparents. The pace of life here is slow and, until the recent troubles in Panama, peaceful.

The weather is always warm, hardly varying from 80 to 85 degrees Fahrenheit all year round. From mid-December to mid-April is the "summer time," the dry season: time for vacations and a break from school for the children. It is a hot season, and a time also for dust and dryness over the hills. From late April through early December is the "winter," or rainy season. Each day during this time one can expect an early afternoon *aguacero,* a brief but intense downpour. The countryside becomes lush and green within days of the beginning of the rains. The dirt roads of the towns and rural areas become pathways of mud, deep and thick. The *quebradas* (ravines) bear torrents of angry water. By October and November the rains are almost constant, and dampness permeates everything. For weeks, it seems, nothing ever dries.

An additional twenty minutes or so past Arraiján, driving west on the Panamerican Highway, one comes across a hardly noticeable, unmarked dirt road off to the left. There is a small shelter for those waiting for the buses that come down the highway, going toward the City. Just off the road is a *cantina,* almost always filled with men sitting around drinking beer and talking. But for the shelter and the small *cantina* one would hardly notice the turn-off.

Neither in the dry nor in the rainy season is this road one for city cars. A jeep or a four-wheel drive pick-up is essential. The road winds back into the hills toward the Pacific Ocean. Dominating the scenery are two mountain peaks: Monte Cabra and Monte Oscuro, Goat Mountain and Dark Mountain. Smaller hills and hollows fill the landscape as one drives down the road deeper into the countryside. The dirt roads are almost always filled with people walking into the interior or out toward the highway. Occasionally one can see small *tiendas,* mom-and-pop stores that sell beer and soda along with a few other basic household items and dried foodstuffs. People stand around the *tiendas* talking, catching up on local news. Usually there is a small group of men talking or singing loudly together, long into an afternoon of drinking. If funds allow, the men might buy a bottle of *seco* together, a strong distilled liquor made of juice from sugar cane. *Seco* is well named: dry as fire and just as hot.

It is the custom for those driving down the road to greet people along the way and to offer a lift to those who are carrying heavy loads. Usually half way down the road the truck or jeep is filled with people, crowded into whatever space is available like tightly crated pineapples off to market. But everyone seems to enjoy the *convivencia,* the instant community within a crowded vehicle, heavy with the heat and wetness of a tropical afternoon and of too many bodies in one small place.

Eventually the dirt road becomes a footpath. But even here, depending on the time of year and the amount of rain, a jeep can continue on into the interior another ten minutes or so. The road, such as it is, goes up and down the small hills, crossing dry ravines or *quebradas* sometimes filled to overflowing with torrents of water. At times the wet red clay of the hillsides is too slippery for travel, and even four-wheel-drive vehicles cannot make the climb. Entry into the heart of the community, then, is by foot.

For the most part the vegetation is lush, more so the deeper we go back into the hills. One can see, from time to time, open areas where corn or rice has been planted, covering spaces where the jungle has been cleared and burned. Small houses called *ranchos,* made of wood planks or bamboo strips, roofed with woven palm branches *(techos de paja,* they are called), can be seen scattered over the hillsides. This is Monte Claro, a small *aldea,* or hamlet, of forty to fifty scattered *ranchos* and 250 or more people. Monte Claro, Clear or Bright Mountain, is indeed a lovely place. High on some of the hills that make up Monte Claro one can see the rich blue of the Pacific Ocean and of the Bay of Panama. Tropical flowers and smells fill every space. Bird sounds of many varieties can be heard as one walks along the dirt pathways. The smell of smoke from nearby wood fires of local kitchens is continually in the air, a reminder that in spite of the rich vegetation and overgrowth, people live here, hidden though they may be at times from view of people walking down the paths. Children play in the stream beds, ever alert for snakes or small crocodiles, which abound here. Early in the morning women can be seen washing clothes or bathing children in the same streams. Most of the men leave the community around sunrise to find their way down the road to the highway, and down the highway to Arraiján or to the City to find a day's work.

These hills and hollows are government property, land set aside by the Agrarian Reform. The people — most of them — are squatters, though a few have obtained deeds from the government for their property. Monte Claro is a new community compared with the neighboring villages. People began coming to this place only fifteen or twenty years ago. They came from the interior provinces of the country looking for a better life. Most of them were and are *campesinos,* rural farmers who lead a traditional or premodern kind of life. In Latin America the word *campesino* is almost synonymous with "peasant." But for the people of Monte Claro the City and its modernism have begun to affect their lives. Long untouched by the influence of urban culture and modern ways, these recently arrived interior folk are struggling with their identity and values. They experience the breakdown of the cohesiveness of their lives and culture, a culture rooted traditionally in the land and in farming and held together by tightly knit extended families. There used to be clear and long-held traditional roles for family members. But now much of this culture of family and land is unravelling before the pressure of urban influence and in the face of the people's inability to survive wholly upon the resources of the land.

Monte Claro is a community in transition. Its instincts are rooted in the *campo,* in the rural areas. More and more its values and sources of income derive from the City. Most adults, especially the men, can neither read nor write. Most of the children can. Men tend to spend days away from the village. The women usually remain. Children, who used to be raised jointly by both parents and by a network of relatives, now are mostly tended to by mothers. Education is available for children ten years old or older, but at a considerable distance from the community. Until recently there were no schools available for the younger children.

There is no electricity in the area, although some of the "better off" members of the community have purchased old television sets, run by automobile batteries. Often neighbors are invited to watch — for a fee. *Novelas,* soap operas, are very popular, picturing the lifestyles of the very rich (and usually troubled) families of far-off places like Mexico City or Caracas. The poorest of the poor rural folk dream of the rich life of the cities, of life they will see first hand only as poorly paid gardeners or laundry women.

Monte Claro, until recently, has been a community almost totally abandoned by every one: by the churches, the government, and even by the surrounding communities. Sickness and malnutrition still abound. Alcoholism among the men is epidemic. There was almost no community organization; every family struggled on its own. There were no schools, no clinics, no churches, no potable water, no electricity, no small stores. Nothing!

Something began to change one day, back in 1985, when a couple of men from the village approached the Episcopal diocese of Panama, through one of the priests in the City, to see if the church could come and offer help to the people of Monte Claro. This invitation to come and see the reality of the people of Monte Claro led eventually to the beginning of a social ministry in the community. Later, when pastoral work had begun, a congregation was started in the heart of the village. It was at that time, late in 1986, that Bethy, a social worker from the diocese, and I started our work together. The Casa Comunal, a community house, was built for the use of the community and its burgeoning organizations. A project was begun to bring in potable water. An elementary school was built and a government teacher obtained. A chapel was constructed, and community groups were organized, with their leaders trained. All of this happened with the combined help of members of the community and with resources offered by the Episcopal Church of Panama, as well as from help given by people from the United States who had become interested in the work of the church in Panama.

The stories shared in this book tell of the life and aspirations of the people of Monte Claro. These are stories of the beginning of a work among an abandoned people, stories of struggle as well as of celebration, descriptions of failure as well as of hope.

In these stories the people speak for themselves. I have changed some of their names, and dialogue has been invented. But this "historical fiction" is true to the reality of the people of Monte Claro. The voices are of real people. The events described, for the most part, are real events. The stories as a whole present a true, flesh-and-blood narrative of Monte Claro.

It should also be noted that the church began its work in Monte Claro during one of the most difficult moments in the history of the Republic of Panama: during the political and economic crisis of 1987–1989, a time of troubles leading up to the tragedy of the U.S. invasion of the Republic of Panama in December of 1989. This reality is woven deeply, if quietly, into the narratives of this book.

The Episcopal Church came by invitation of the community to share its life and to bring some Good News where there had been mostly passivity and hopelessness. Those of us who worked among the people of Monte Claro came to serve in several distinct ways. We were concerned not to come in ways that would dominate or control the life of

the community. But rather we came trying to work along-
side the people, to learn from them as well as to offer what
we had.

Three strategies describe our way of trying to be among
the *monteclareños*. First, we came to help the community
understand its reality more clearly. Together we pursued an
analysis that could enable the community, in the light of its
common faith, to make choices and plans that could affect its
future. Ours was a ministry of helping a people to be aware
of and to understand the reality of their world, a reality that
both oppressed them and opened up possibilities for a more
just and hopeful life. This was the work of *concientización*,
of the kind of raising of awareness that could lead to action
for change.

We also came out of compassion. We came not out of the
kind of compassion that offers a benevolent, condescending
charity. But we tried to discover a way of compassion that
could be mutual among us. It was a compassion that could
lead to accompaniment, to walking with a people in their
journey toward hope and transformation. It was a kind of
solidaridad with the people, a sharing as much as possible
both of powerlessness as well as of emerging strength.

Lastly, we came to participate in the empowerment of
people. We came to help organize and train the people of
Monte Claro so that they could better determine their own
future, identify their own needs, and arrive at their own solutions. We came for the *capacitación*, the enablement of
people, so that strength could replace dependency in the
ways we would struggle for life and for our future.

It is hoped that the following stories can give North
Americans an opportunity to know something of the cur-
rents of faith and hope running through parts of the church

in Latin America. It is my hope that sharing these stories, memories true to the experience of a people of faith and emerging from the cauldron where struggle generates the possibility of liberation, can help to widen the community of understanding between North and South.

It is also my conviction that one of the important dynamics of the movement of reform and liberation in the Latin American church is that of the growth and importance of "local theologies": that is, of theological expression that emerges from the experience and reflection of people within their local context (what in Latin America is referred to as "base communities"). This is a theology that emerges especially among the poor and powerless from whom traditionally we have not expected a voice of clarity or of hope. The "localization" or "contextualization" of theology is nothing new. In fact many argue that it was the original form of theology in the early generations of the church. But after centuries of the academic and hierarchical captivity of theology, new movements are emerging. This is true especially among Christians of the Two-thirds World, where local communities are encouraged to reflect on the Gospel in the light of their own unique experience. These local communities do this reflection not out of mere curiosity, but out of a passionate concern to learn what it is they are called to *do* as Christians, how it is that they can work together toward liberation from all that victimizes them. This is theology "from below," a voice from the voiceless of the centuries. This is theology inclusive of the whole context of a people's reality and ways of knowing, freed from the hegemony of reason alone. I hope that these stories might give a sense of how that reflection happens, of how understanding and action flow from a community when people are set free and encouraged to be theologians, to be for themselves a source of the prophetic voice of God.

Local theologizing is an exciting endeavor, but not without its times of tension and confusion. What happens, for example, when authority is grounded in the roots of the community rather than above or beyond it? What is the role of "popular religion" among people, of faith and practices that the church has at times believed to be full of "superstition"? How does one make room for the deep wisdom of the Spirit among a people who have their own way of seeing and hearing? How much of our own Northern and Anglo cultural and historical agenda do we impose unknowingly on these communities, agenda that inhibit this process of hearing the Word of God "in a new key"? And how do we enable "local theologies" to connect with other streams of time and geography where the Good News has been heard and responded to? While these stories may not give many answers to such questions, they will share something of the birthpangs of a people trying to deal with them, people trying to become believable signs of the reign of God in a place known mostly for its scarcity of hope.

There is a song from the *Misa salvadoreña* (Salvadoran Mass) that is popular among Central American Christians. It says:

> *Cuando el pobre cree en el pobre,*
> *ya podremos cantar libertad ...*

> When the poor believe in themselves,
> we will be able to sing of liberation ...

The stories that follow — voices and thoughts of a remarkable group of *monteclareños* — are about the planting of the first seeds of this believing and singing. And these stories, too, are about what the poor have to give to us who are otherwise rich.

•

NOTE: Throughout these stories a variety of Spanish words and phrases are used. Sometimes they are used because the Spanish simply does not translate well. Many times, however, Spanish is used to enable what we in Panama would call *el sabor,* the flavor of the story, to emerge. Most of the time the context will help you understand what is being said.

To help readers unfamiliar with Spanish a small glossary of words and phrases used in these stories can be found at the back of the book.

CUENTOS
PANAMEÑOS

ONE

MARI
The Chicken Project

I ALWAYS like to get up before dawn, before my children and
my husband, Chan, are awake. Sometimes it is the only
moment during the day I have to myself. I love these times
of quiet each day, though in a sense they are not very quiet,
for long before sunrise the many birds of our *finca* begin to
sing. I have almost memorized all of their songs. The one I
like the best has a short, beautiful song, a chant-like *saloma*.
I don't know the bird's name, but I call it *la enamorada*, the
woman in love. Her song reminds me of the love songs I've
always wanted to hear.

In the early morning hours I can see through the siding
of my *rancho*, through the cracks of the bamboo walls. I can
see the beginning of each new day. It is faint at first, but I'm
used to looking carefully. When the stars are just right, and
the glow above the far hill is just so, then I know it is time
for me to get up. I can feel it within me as well as see it. And
that is why I like the early morning hours.

> *Buenos días, día.*
> *Con Dios me acuesto,*

con Dios me levanto
a la bienaventurada
y al espíritu santo.

I greet the day.
With God I lie down,
and with God I rise
to the Blessed Virgin
and to the Holy Spirit.

Before Chan and the children wake I start the fire on the *fogón*. I like to hear it crackle and to smell the smoke as it cuts through the early morning coolness. Chan also likes coffee when he awakes. I like to do good things for him. Most of the time he is good to me. He works hard. Does not drink too much. He doesn't abuse me or the children like the other men do in their homes. I wouldn't let him. I would run away before I'd allow him to treat me like Emelina's man treats her. But she has family nearby to run to. I don't.

Anyway Chan treats me well. He has given me six children already — *mis bendiciones,* my blessings, I call them — and I'm only twenty-six years old. I still look young, thank God. But I think I have enough children. Chan won't hear of me fixing it so that I can't have more children. He won't even talk about it; he says it isn't the way God meant things. I think though that one day I will decide to do something so that I won't have more babies. Chan will be mad for a while, but he'll come around. He doesn't stay mad at me very long. And I will do things quietly. Chan's honor in the village is important, and I don't want to humiliate him. At the clinic they will demand my husband's permission. But I know the woman at the clinic; she'll arrange things for me, *si Dios quiere,* if God wills.

Today Bethy comes to meet again with the women of the community. She comes from the diocesan office in the City, and I think of her as my friend. We are trying to get together a cooperative, a project for raising chickens to sell outside the community. We know how to raise yard chickens; *Dios mío,* we have done this since we can remember. But Bethy and Padre have brought two men from the university who say that we can raise chickens with more meat and raise them in the wet season. People here believe you can't raise chickens in the rainy season, but we'll see.

Mostly Bethy wants to help organize the women of the village so that their life will be better. I laugh when I hear the way she describes the men here: in her characteristic way and with sparkle in her eye she calls them *bien flojos* — ineffectual, lazy, undependable. She is partly right, but she doesn't always understand. Our men are beaten and humiliated by life outside the village. It's because most of them have to go to the City each day to find work, and there they are treated poorly. People in the City think that *campesinos* are dumb and weak. True we do not have much education. But our men are very clever. And they work hard, doing things that no city man would do. An *urbano* would never be a *machetero* all day in the hot sun.

But almost always our men experience humiliation in the City. They are treated like children. People laugh at their simple dress and make fun of their ways of speaking. They often treat them as invisible people, look right through them, talk right past them. Chan says it makes him boil inside like *sancocho.* But he keeps quiet and answers with his broad smile. It's the only way.

I think that we women of Monte Claro have it better than the men. We at least can stay in the village, have our life

here, follow our customs, and care for our children. Our men, however, have to live both as *campesinos* and as urban people. They have to know both worlds. Many of them begin to look down on their traditions, their life in the *campo*. They see the cars, the radios, the TVs, and the wealth of the City. They dream of it for themselves and for their families. But I think it is a bad dream. We'll never get these things, so why get all torn up trying to dream of them. Yes, our men are torn up and divided inside. And that's why I think they drink so much at the end of the day. They are sad and confused, and angry sometimes at the way we *campesinos* are treated. I'm glad I can stay here in Monte Claro most of the time. I feel sorry for Chan and his friends.

But Bethy is right. I think that the women here are more ready than the men to organize and to try to better the lives of their families. So we have begun working on this chicken project. It takes cooperation and for the most part we do that fairly well. The women look up to me as a leader, and I like that. I'm younger than most, but I can read and write, and

I have good ideas. Many of the women here feel that they can't think. They are only for having babies and for cooking. That's what some of their men tell them. But Bethy is trying to help us see ourselves differently. We have our projects, we have our small treasury, and we are learning how to be more in charge of our lives.

Bethy gets impatient with us at times. She complains to us about our timidity, about our unwillingness to learn new things. She says we are like children, like *muñecos* (dolls) in the hands of our men, in the hands of the rich, and in the hands of the government. Though she gets very frustrated at times, we know she really cares about us. She keeps saying that *campesinas* are women of dignity, of beauty, and of a wealth of traditions far better than the values of the women of the cities who only know how to dream about a pretty dress or a TV to watch the *novelas*. I too dream of having a pretty dress, but I agree with her. We need to learn that we can be proud women who know how to live and survive better than most people.

I think that we all listen to Bethy and love her because she too grew up in the *campo*. She was born and raised in the countryside in El Salvador, and she knows our ways. We trust her; and if we fight with her it is because we are *compañeras*, we are sisters. And we know she likes to be with us.

I don't know Padre Ricardo as well as I do Bethy. But I think he values us as women. He treats us at least with more respect than we are used to. I am surprised at times when he asks for our opinions, just as he asks for those of the men. But I am still getting to know him.

I remember one time when Padre asked me to read the lesson at the Mass. I was very proud. I read well and like to have the chance to participate in this way. Well, time came for the reading. I had Marcelita on my lap. She is only ten months old and was very hungry. So before I read I unbuttoned my dress and gave her my breast so she could drink. Then I started to read: *"Como pastor, lleva a pastar a su rebano, toma en brazos a los corderos, los pone junto a su corazón, y conduce al reposo a las paridas."* "Like a shepherd God will tend the flock, and with arms will keep them together; God will carry the lambs near the bosom and lead the ewes to water." I had to remain seated as I read; but that didn't seem to matter. I was very happy doing two things that for me were beautiful. And Padre seemed happy too. That's why I think he respects women. I also notice how he relates to Bethy when they work together. It is so different from the way our men treat us here.

These past few weeks I have been very sad and worried. Chan is discouraged and doesn't talk with me much. I know it is because he too is afraid. He has a good job with the Ministry of Public Works, working on the roads in the area of Arraiján. But recently there has not been much to do as the government has run out of money and materials. Bethy says it is because of the *gringos* who have stopped money from coming into Panama. I asked Padre Ricardo about this. He told me that the United States is against the government of General Noriega and is trying to get him out of power. One way they can do this is to make the government suffer for lack of money. I think that it is the people like us who suffer. Padre tells us that for years the United States has treated Panama as a child, as someone to protect and control. Now Panama is trying to take care of itself, to be independent. It seems very much like the way things are in Monte Claro. Some people have all the power and all the wealth. Others suffer without much of either. The wealthy and powerful in the City seem to treat us poor as simply people useful to them at times. We do the dirty work. They get the benefits. Padre says this is not God's will. God longs for justice for all people, not just for a few. And so I think that the United States is treating Panama like the rich of the City treat *campesinos:* as *muñecos*.

The result of all of this is that Chan has not been paid for almost a month. The government has given him checks, but no one will take them, or if they do, they pay him only a small part of what they are worth. So he cashes them, but for so little. What else can he do? Some haven't even been able to do that. "So I guess we're lucky," he says. But I can see in his eyes, by his silence that he doesn't believe what he says. He is just trying to make me feel better. But I am sad and afraid for we can't live like this. We are hungry a lot of the time now. Last night Chan came home very late. He was drunk, but I didn't say anything. I knew he was very sad.

It is like this for most of us in Monte Claro. Everyone is having a hard time. It is still the rainy season, and we have more sicknesses this time of year. There is not much food from the land because it is still too wet, still several months away from harvest. I pray every time at the *misa* that God will look down and see how we suffer. Padre says that God does care, that God too suffers with us. For me that's a strange idea: that God suffers. But we have talked together about *solidaridad,* about how sharing each other's troubles makes them more bearable. We have found this out a little bit in working together as women. When we share our troubles we are less afraid. We really do help each other. Maybe that's the way it is with God. God sees and knows our struggles. God walks with us in them. God helps us to be more of a community, more like sisters and brothers together, so that no one need struggle alone. We sing a song that says *Cristo vive en la solidaridad*, Christ lives in our solidarity. These are all such new ideas for me. My head spins with it all sometimes. But somehow inside me I feel that what we are learning now is more true than what we have learned in the past, more hopeful.

Yesterday was a very disappointing day for me. I had worked for three months raising chickens in the women's group chicken project. Even Chan got interested and helped me. At first he was distant and skeptical. But little by little he got excited about the possibilities. That made me very happy. We watched the chickens grow fast with the grain we fed them, and Chan learned how to vaccinate to prevent disease. I've never seen chickens grow so fast, so plump. We were told we could get a good price for them at the markets. So came the day to sell them. We had to sell quickly because the feed was costing us a lot. Yesterday we learned that there were too many chickens just now in the City. The markets would only offer us a fraction of the price we had hoped for. Among all the women of the village there were about five hundred chickens ready for sale. But no one would buy them unless we sold them cheaply. So we did. Chan and I had counted on the extra money. We had spent it in our minds several times over. But at least we got our money back.

Chan was not as discouraged as I. He says, "Look, we have learned something! We have a real chicken house, we know how to feed them, and we know how to vaccinate. Next time will be better!" Next time! Yes, I want to do this again if we can get the money, *si Dios quiere*. We keep hoping, Chan and I.

Padre and Bethy were sad too, but we cheered them up.

"Look, *compañeros,*" we said, "this is not the first time we've been disappointed. We'll try again. Like you tell us, God has not abandoned us; God will help us learn to work as a community. And it's been true. We women have learned better how to work together. And Chan and I have shared in a family project, one that has given us hope. So it wasn't totally a failure. We have to keep trying; no one can do it for us." At least that is how we tried to cheer them up. And I believe in what we said — mostly.

My, how my mind runs and runs! These thoughts come to me each morning when I am alone. They are not just thoughts from today, but from many mornings like this one. Ay, how full my heart is sometimes! How rich are my dreams!

Chan's pig is beginning to make a lot of noise. If he is not careful he will wake up everyone. Except for old *gordito,* the fat one, all is still and quiet. It has been a good early morning for me.

> *Con Dios me acuesto,*
> *con Dios me levanto . . .*
>
> With God I lie down,
> and with God I rise . . .

I like it when I can think and remember inside me like I have this morning. It's the way I pray. For a while I feel free and beautiful. I like my family, my home and community, for all its suffering and troubles. But I like too to be able to escape from time to time, to dream about other things that are true. I like being with myself this way. *La enamorada* must like it too, for she has just flown by again with her beautiful song. She's gone for the day, but she'll be back tomorrow. So will I.

TWO

GISELA
A Poem

A child walks
along the sand,
and up the clay-cracked path
silent among her
thoughts.

She throws a pebble
over the water,
and skips a stone over the tops
of the *plátano* trees.

She stares into
the open tropical sky
without expression, without hint
of her hard-held secrets.

And she listens to the
absurd song
of the jacamar,
and thinks to herself
"How lovely,

how crazy the beauty
of this moment
held dear
in the heat of the day."

Nothing connects
and nothing will
in the song
of her wild friend,
and yet she smiles
because just now
it doesn't matter.

She smiles with the recognition
that beauty is
so free and unmanageable,
so unable to play
but the comic
in the midst
of all her serious
concerns.

The child
with her old woman's
wrinkled heart,
pressed like a hardened path
by her brief years,
moves on,
on past lightness,
past the moment of childhood
heard in the jacamar's call,
on to her *ranchito,*
filled with returning

to what won't be,
filled with the dormant reminders
which have been awakened
for a moment
in her hearing
of the jacamar.

THREE

DON PACÍFICO
The Healer

S OMETIMES my head is full to bursting with memories. Sometimes it is like a cupped hand trying to carry water from the *quebrada* to the house. What little is held slips away so fast I can barely retain it. I'm getting old, I guess. Humph! Old, I say: I'm withered and dry like an old *sombrero* blowing in the wind, sweat-stained and tattered, worn too many days.

I am old, somewhere between eighty and a hundred years. Why such a rough guess? It's a game I play when people ask me how old I am. I smile and mumble something they can't understand; then they will have to ask again. And I laugh and tell them some figure, some guess. I tell other people something else; so everyone has a different idea of how old I am. The truth is I don't know.

I was born in the interior province of Coclé, in a place up in the hills called Quebrada Angosta, narrow ravine. My family, who didn't keep records, had lived there as long as memory could imagine. We were *campesinos,* traditional folk who lived off the land raising mostly corn and rice. We knew also how to raise cattle, pigs, chickens, and whatever else we could find to grow and eat, and sometimes sell. We seldom went down the hill to the towns; almost never to the City. We were usually self-sufficient. But I remember times when the harvest was bad for lack of rain. My father and uncles would go down to the province of Herrera to work in the sugar cane fields for a few months. But the work was very hard and the pay little. None of our people liked to work for the *finqueros,* the ranchers who demanded a lot and paid little. Our men were proud and hated the humiliations they endured working as *peones* in the fields.

¡Ay, Dios! I have a mountain of memories hidden inside me. Memory is a good thing when you're old and blind like I am. Memory is a *chacara* (woven bag) filled with colors, smells, and sounds, stuffed full with people and events. Who needs to see when memory is so rich? I feel sad for myself only when my memory fades, when it is asleep and I can't bring it to life again. In those moments I am very lonely. But most of the time my blindness is a gift. I hear and smell and touch my world more deeply than others, for I experience things others miss in the busyness of daily work. They think they see. But, ha!, they miss almost everything.

My blindness usually does not keep me from remembering. I can still sit outside on a warm, dark summer night and feel the weight of stars above me. Or I can sit in the shade of the giant *huipo* tree and feel its grand canopy of leaves far above me.

I even see spirits and angels and *santos.* Not in the way you see a frog or a parrot, but in the way you see things of the other world, in the way you see God. I am a *curandero,* a healer. And I hope to be so until I die, *si Dios quiere.* Not as many people come to me now as in years past. That's all

right with me, really. I'm too tired to do all the things I used
to do. But it makes me sad that my people do not believe in
the ways of the *curandero*.

I have a gift. It's not mine, really; it was passed on to me
by my uncle in Coclé, Tío Romero. He received the gift from
someone in his family, I don't know who it was. I have always
believed that though the gift comes through someone in the
family, it truly comes from God, from the Holy Spirit within
us. And so I have given away freely what I have received. No
one should pay for the gifts of God, *¿Verdad?*

I know in my head all about the herbs and roots that cure,
about all the mixtures of juices and potions we have used for
centuries. And I know the rituals too; but sometimes I don't
know why we perform this ritual or that. Their meanings
have been lost somewhere down the years. I know a lot inside me, enough to fill a book if I could write. But people
are losing interest in the *curanderos,* losing sight of a way to
live in God's world, a world where everything we touch can
be sacred. I may end up being the last *curandero* in Monte
Claro. *¡Qué lástima!* What a pity!

People come to me, most of them, when all else fails. *¡Ay,
Dios mío!* I'm not a magician — only a simple man who happens to have the gift. I can help people with our traditional
ways, but only if they come to me early on. God's earth is
filled with good things, things that bring joy and that bring
healing. I use what comes from the sacred earth.

And faith! You've got to have faith in God and in the
saints. Sometimes I think that faith in God is more important than all the herbs, leaves, roots, and barks I use. Often
people don't get well because of all the turmoil inside them.
How can they heal their bodies when their *alma* is so troubled? Ha! I told Padre once that I have lived so long because

Bird of Paradise plant

when I was young I ate *tigre,* the meat of tigers. I meant that as a joke, but only partly. Maybe the soul of the *tigre* is really in me, and that's the way God gives me strength to live so long. Maybe the *tigre* inside me is the source of my calmness and peace, as well as of my energy. I don't know, but *gracias a Dios* I am alive, and I have been blessed by a large family.

People often call me a holy man. Perhaps. I think in a way I am a holy man. Not good, especially, but holy, *¿No?* That is, I'm just a poor *campesino,* a humble man who has done all the things, good and bad, that others before me have done. But because of my gift I remind people of the holiness of God's earth, of the trees and streams, the birds and dogs, the sun and the rain — all of it holy! The other day after watching my son Chan kicking his pig in anger, old *chancho* who had broken into a bag of *maíz,* and had eaten all of it . . . that day I said to Chan, "*Hijo,* son, go easy, even old *gordito* is holy!" Chan was too mad to laugh.

Chan has been a good son to me. It has been about ten

years or so that he sent for me, brought me from Coclé to Monte Claro. He wanted to be able to take care of me here. At first I didn't want to leave, but it had to be, *¿No?* I had so little family left in Coclé. Here the hills are laced with little seeds of mine, with sons and daughters, grandchildren, nieces and nephews. *Dios mío,* what have I caused?

I live with Fidelina, my *sobrina,* my niece. She and her husband live with their four small children on the top of the hill overlooking the new chapel in Monte Claro. It's a long climb to the top, but I do it almost every day. My feet know by heart every clod, every rock on the path. With my cane and my memory I can walk almost anywhere in the village. I go alone most of the time, with only my dog Chocho to accompany me.

Fidelina and her family are good to me, but the children, *¡Ay, Dios!* they wear me out. So on days when there is not too much rain or mud, I walk down to Chan and Mari's *rancho,* sit on a stool in the open place in front of the house, with a palm roof over me to keep out the sun or the rain, and I greet people as they come by. I can sit like that for hours. Chan's house is on one of the main pathways of the village, so almost all of my friends come by each day. Many times they stop to talk, to tell me of the news of the day or of their problems. I listen but don't say much except, "*Qué Jesucristo te bendiga,* May Jesus bless you." Sometimes Mari will bring coffee to us. It's not coffee from real coffee beans, but rather it is made from the seed pods of the *saril* bush. It looks and tastes like coffee, almost. And it's what we have. *Saril* grows all over our hillsides.

I don't drink *seco.* A long time ago in Coclé I was part of a small Pentecostal group in our mountains. They were very strict about not drinking. They were strict about a lot of things. But they were also full of joy. We knew how to sing, how to praise Jesus, and how to take good care of each other. *¡Ay!* such singing and carrying on. For hours on a Sunday afternoon we would sing and shout. I loved it.

But since coming to Monte Claro I have been going to the *misa* of the Episcopal Church. It is more like I was used to as a child. And Padre has brought some good songs with him. He plays guitar, or someone else in the village plays, and we sing and sing. At first our people were shy about singing. They didn't know the words, and most couldn't read the little books he brought. But now we know all the songs, and sing like real *coclesanos* with the fire and joy of the people in the mountains where I came from. I used to swing my arms in the air as I sang. But I'm too old and stiff to do that now; so I do it inside me. There is still some *Pentecostal* in me.

The song that we sing here, the one I like most, is a song that makes me want to dance. I call it my *Aleluya* song:

> *Gracias por el amor del cielo,*
> *gracias por el inmenso mar,*
> *gracias por el cantar del bosque,*
> *Aleluya.*

> Thank you for heaven's love,
> thank you for the vast sea,
> thank you for the song of the forest,
> Alleluia.

Sometimes I forget the words, but I can always sing the Alleluia.

On some days when there is not too much rain, and she is in a good mood, Mari gets a fire going and makes *sancocho* for everyone. Most people think of *sancocho* as our national dish. Mari, I think, makes the best. She gets out her *paila*, a huge iron pot, and fills it with water, *yuca*, baby corn, *culantro*, *yame*, rice, and (if we have it) chicken. It boils and boils until the smell of *culantro* and chicken fills the patio. Then by late afternoon, when the men are coming down the path after a hot day of work, we have an unannounced fiesta. *¡Que sabrosa!* What wonderful flavor! With bowls of *sancocho* we talk into the night, solving all the problems of the community. Many times Padre and Bethy join us.

I have not been feeling well lately. I'm very weak and need a lot of people to take care of me. I hate it when my body reminds me that I am an old man. Last week I was in bed almost every day. On Sunday, when Padre was here for the *misa*, I fainted, or at least that's what Mari said. Chan rushed to get someone with a truck to carry me to the clinic in Arraiján, a short way down the road from Monte Claro. He was very worried about me.

Chan left me at the clinic and came back to Monte Claro to tell Padre Ricardo where I was, so that Padre could bring me back later. *¡Ay, Dios mío!* I was very confused and didn't know what was happening to me. The doctor at the clinic sent me by taxi to the hospital in Panama City, thirty minutes or so away. When Padre and Mari came in his jeep to find me, I wasn't at the clinic and no one knew for sure where I was. The doctor had gone home. After checking around they found someone who thought that I had been taken to Santo Tomás hospital. So off they went to the City.

Eventually they found me in the emergency room of the hospital. Catalino, my *primo* in Monte Claro, was with me. The people at the hospital said that I had pneumonia and gave me some medicine and told me to stay in bed. I didn't have any money so I couldn't stay at the hospital. Anyway

I would rather be back at Fidelina's house. So Padre, Mari, and Catalino lifted me up and carried me to the jeep for the ride back to Monte Claro. It was late by now and very dark.

We met Chan waiting for us on the road into the interior of the village. The road was too muddy for the jeep to enter any further, so Chan had to carry me. *¡Ay, chuleta!* There I was a grown man being hoisted up onto Chan's back. My own son, the one I brought into this world, carried me like a *burrito*. Shoeless and sloshing through the mud, he carried me up and down the hills. If it weren't so pathetic I would have laughed. I was too weak to do or say anything.

Well, I'm feeling better now. Padre has come to visit and pray with me. Ha! Padre comes to heal a *curandero*. *Bueno,* I thank holy Jesus for whatever help comes to me. *"¡Ay! Señor cura,"* I say to Padre, "maybe there are days when I am *padre* to you."

FOUR

VICTOR
Longing and
Resistance

I DIDN'T know that learning to hope again would make me so afraid." I was deep into these thoughts as I walked down the muddy road to find the bus for the City. I ignored the red clay sticking to my old shoes, clinging like the weight of troubled thoughts. I am young and considered by many to be a leader in the community. But I'm struggling. I do not want to go where I think someone is pulling me. My fear is not the immobilizing, shattering kind, but more like a slow gnawing within me, like a dry ache after a night of too much *seco*.

I don't think Padre Ricardo understands the fear we feel. He is passionate about our future and gets discouraged when we back off from this desire to dream. He pushes when we are passive and seem not to care. I too want to dream, but I don't believe much will change. It never has, and I can't see how it will.

I met Padre Ricardo four months ago when members of

the diocesan office in the City came to introduce the new team that will be working with us in the small community of Monte Claro, Arraiján. The Episcopal Church has been working in this community of *campesinos* for about a year and has finally come to a place where a diocesan team could be committed to the task of community support and development. Sra. Bethy and Srta. Glenda provide leadership for community social projects, and Padre does pastoral work and helps with educational programs for leadership training and community organization. To me it all seems interesting, but also a bit overwhelming. So I sit light to it all, not sure if I want to risk myself for something that might pass with noise and fury like an afternoon downpour, but that evaporates just as surely in the tropical heat. I am frankly as sceptical as I am anxious.

Padre is definitely cultivating me, urging me to take responsibility, wanting me to commit myself to the well-being of the community more than simply to my own interests. We walk together often, Padre and I, sometimes down to the beach, at other times through the lush hillsides on which are scattered the *ranchos* and *fincas* of my people. Padre's Spanish is weak at times, but he tries. And I understand all too much what he wants of me. But life is hard here and the people don't want to do anything. "Why should I work my ass off for people who don't want to change?" I thought as I approached the small store, Santa María, to buy some rice and coffee for my woman, Lidia. At the window of the small shop stood Florenzio and Catalino, *bien borracho*, drunk as usual these days. They are my friends with whom I have laughed, fought, and drunk. These are the men I would have to depend on if I were to take seriously Ricardo and Bethy's concern to work for change in Monte Claro. So, they haven't got any work! What's new? Everyone struggles for a little rice and *yuca* on the plate these days. And with the current crisis in Panama there are fewer jobs. They've all dried up like the wretched summer dust, and friends like Flores and Cata are depressed. Together with a bottle of *seco* they will dream dreams, dance free and light, and end up the night in the mud along the road somewhere, their women quietly cursing God for this bitter life, sad for having brought yet more children into it, into the mud-spewn, hollow-stomached, alcohol stench of it all. Monte Claro is a shit hole, I think at times.

Don Tino, the *alcalde* of Monte Claro told me one day how this village came to be. Tino was mayor by default; no one else wanted the job, and he had been around Monte Claro the longest. Poor man, Don Tino cares about his people but is paralyzed like the rest in the face of apathy and *egoismo.* "You look out for yourself if you want to survive," most people think. Tino would occasionally have spurts of energy when he would try to organize a *fiesta* or pull together a work party for a community project. But again and again he would be beaten down by the bickering, the lack of dependability of the people, and the enormity of the task. But Tino did not give up easily. Padre first met him when he was long into a bottle of *Abuelo,* the local bargain-priced rum. Things had not been going well for him. But usually he was steady and dependable, if a bit swamped by thick sadness: "very depressed," he often described himself.

Tino told me that people started coming to these hills about twenty years ago, coming from the interior, from Los Santos and Herrera and Coclé to find a better life near the City. Well, it hasn't yet happened, this better life. It's a generation later and we still struggle like dung beetles to make it through the week. Most of the families are related, *primos* and *sobrinos*. That's good in times of crisis. But also it is the cause of much battling in the community. You can count on at least one family *lucha* going on at any time.

But people came, year by year, until there were over 40 families and 250 people living scattered over the hills of Monte Claro. And among all of these families there are probably only four or five men who have steady work. So much for our last attempt to dream! When there is work it is mostly day labor as *macheteros*, cleaning fields with machetes, backbreaking work I wouldn't give to a dog. We are paid only five dollars or so a day and think we are lucky to have this pittance!

Our women usually stay at home. A few sometimes venture out to do domestic work. But who will take care of the kids? And besides most domestic work pays so little, and our women have to run constantly from the young men of the house who always want to get up their skirts. That's no life!

When Padre and Bethy came to us there was no potable water, no roads passable in the rainy season, no school, and no church. The government didn't know we were here, or better pretended not to notice except around election time. *Gracias a Dios* we don't have many elections! We were abandoned people, abandoned by our own despair and fatalism as much as by the church and the government. But we are tough, and we are still here. In my area some of the houses are made of cinderblock. But deeper into the community the poor bastards live knee deep in mud for nine months of the year, in houses made of bamboo and palm, full of vermin and bugs. But at least the countryside is beautiful with some of the prettiest hills in the area. And the *puesta del sol*, the sunsets here, are the most lovely anywhere. Too bad we can't market them!

Most of us try to farm a bit: *yuca*, corn, some rice, some fruit, *guandu*. And always there are *pollos de patio*, ragged chickens running about everywhere eating bugs and leaving their shit on the kitchen floor. Chan down the road has tried to grow pigs. But they usually get sick on him. There is no getting ahead in all of this. The more you try, the harsher is the disappointment. But occasionally there is a spurt of creative energy, a *ranchito* rebuilt, a *finca* enlarged, a project planned. *¡Jesús María!* the people just can't be completely put down. That's what Ricardo keeps saying. But he has more experience than I.

Don't get me wrong. I'm glad Padre and Bethy are here. Things are a better now. At least someone seems to care about us. We have plans now for an aqueduct, a water line into the village that will give us good water several times a week. The school for our little ones is being built, and land for a chapel has been donated by the community. It is all very slow: one step forward, a dozen backward.

Padre Ricardo and Bethy tell us that we have to do the work. They won't do anything for us that we can do for ourselves. They say that they want to help us to be self-sufficient, to avoid more dependencies, which eventually lead to deeper powerlessness. So things go very slowly. I know I don't carry my full share. I'm ashamed of that. But I can't help myself. People say that "Victor is all talk, no follow-through." *Habla mucho pero sin caminar.* I hate it when people say that to me, even when it is true.

My mother, Marcelina, is a saint. She looks very old for her years. Who wouldn't be after raising four boys like us, and with a *flojo* for a father, more absent than present: often *better* absent than present. Mama is small, light as a *paloma*'s feather, shriveled and dry except for her heart. But she's tough. And sad. Sad for the way her boys have turned out. Sad for the divisions in the community. Sad for the years of poverty and the harshness of work. She is very religious. And she loves Padrecito. He often comes in the afternoon to have a cup of coffee in her kitchen before doing some visits. He comes to hear her version of life in Monte Claro week by week, her analysis, he calls it. Padre is big on analysis. He also comes, I think, because she mothers him a bit. He comes because he knows she cares for the community even though she too has little hope.

They sit and talk in her little kitchen, a palm-thatched *ranchito* at the side of her house, with a clay floor and a couple of rickety stools. He likes the smell of the fire in the *fogón,* the raised table covered with dirt and clay where she keeps her fire. He enjoys her storytelling and her laughter, the lightness of heart she keeps even after all these years. Marcelina is one of the most respected women in the community, but she often keeps her distance from it for the criticism and pain she bears because of her sons. *¡Ay, Mamacita,* how hard it is for you. I'm glad Padre and Bethy have become your friends.

Padre has asked me to serve as junior warden of the newly organized mission of San Isidro Labrador, St. Isidore of Madrid, *campesino* and worker. I feel honored, but also feel unworthy of his trust. I will fail him as I have failed my mother and my people. I try to tell him so. But he says he believes in me and already knows my limitations. I too want the church to be strong here. We need it. I need it. But does Padre really know how weak I am? That I flirt with Aurelia hoping my *señora* won't know? That I didn't use the money he gave me to help the family down the road whose house had burnt? That I "borrowed" it for myself and now can't pay it back? Does he know that I know how undependable I am, that I talk a big line but deliver little? Sometimes I just don't show for meetings when I know he counts heavily on my being there. "It's not me you let down, Victor," he often says. "It's the people, your *compañeros* here in Monte Claro." Still he believes in me. Still he tries to help me become better. Sometimes I wish he wouldn't try. Often Bethy is so angry with me she tells me to "Go to hell." She's a tough, no nonsense *salvadoreña*. I wish Padre would be tough with me sometimes. But usually he asks for me to try again. I know I make him sad.

But I'm not just a failure in what matters to me. For several years I have been the "sheriff" of Monte Claro, appointed by the Junta Comunal of Arraiján. My job is to keep the peace here and to try to keep out the *ladrones,* the thieves who come into Monte Claro from other villages. I do that well, and people respect me for it. I even got beaten up several weeks ago by a man I turned in for fighting while drunk. He beat me up something good, but now, for a while, I'm a hero in the community.

Last night at the meeting of the Junta Misionera we had a discussion on a Bible reading from one of the Gospels, I don't remember which. Almost everyone came to the meeting, members and curious on-lookers alike. Even old Don Pacífico, blind as his ancient dog, came shuffling up the dirt path to the Casa Comunal, followed by his mangy bitch. He had hoped we were going to celebrate a *misa,* but remained with us for a while anyway.

It was a good meeting. Everyone participated. And Padre's Spanish was better than usual. Mari, Chan's *señora,*

read the story about the time when Peter and John asked Jesus secretly for privileged positions in the Kingdom. Those bastards really tried to pull one over on the rest of their friends. But they got found out. We shared our ideas about the reading. Padre and Bethy say that we can all be good theologians when we share honestly about our lives and about what we hear in the Bible.

We talked about being "lorded over" by almost everyone. As *campesinos* we are at the bottom of almost everyone's shit pile. We are authorities at being "lorded over." But too we know how to "lord it over" each other. Here in the community we are continually fighting for power, for a bigger slice of what there is, for influence. Padre said that perhaps the harshest way we oppress ourselves is by our *individualismo,* our not caring about the community but only looking out for ourselves. It's true, we are not much of a community at times, and we get beaten down because of that. We talked a long time last night about our community, about what keeps us down. Bethy and Padre told us that they come to work *among* us, to work *with* us and not *over* us. That is why they almost always refuse to make decisions for us. Often that infuriates the community, for we are used to someone "lording it over" us. We don't know what to do when someone takes us seriously, expecting us to take responsibility together for our own decisions. *Mutualidad* is a word we often use.

Jesus, in the story that was read, told his disciples to turn everything upside down. It is in giving of yourself, in serving the community that you find power. Alone, separately we keep getting lost in the mud. Together we have power, we have possibilities. We don't have to wait for the government, or even for the church, waiting like pitiful children with our eyes cast down.

Padre and Bethy come to our community without fail. They come in the storms when the mud pathways are barely passable. Often the people say "They won't come for Mass today, the weather is too bad." But they always come. Padre, the rich *gringo*, comes without fail. He's been baptized time and again by the damned Monte Claro mud. In those times, mud-spattered, he looks like one of us. We're beginning to believe that the church will stick with us. So we are not just the receivers of some bit of charity that will dry up when the sun comes out, or when the church finds that the people here move very slowly.

Sometimes I think that Padre and I are in different worlds, worlds too far apart to bridge: like the other day, after a monster storm when the *quebrada* (the stream) was so full we couldn't cross. I was on one side, Padre on the other. We stood there helplessly for over an hour. Then with a chain of hands we were able to help him across. But I felt sad, felt so distant. He can't really know what it is like for us. He tries, and he does better than most. At times he thinks he understands, and doesn't. No one tells him; they simply say yes to everything. At times he knows he can't cross the bridge, but wants to be with us anyway. He says that's acceptance. He wants to accept me as I am. He wants to be accepted even as a crazy *gringo*. And he wants us to begin to accept one another, as *hermanos,* as *compañeros* on the same road, as followers of brother Jesus.

It's no wonder I am afraid at times. We are all afraid. Afraid as much for our own limitations as we are afraid of Bethy and Padre giving up on us, of God giving up on us. I try to believe God is not punishing us by making us so poor. But I often feel we deserve God's anger. Padre says no. But at those times I think that Padre Ricardo does not understand how we feel.

FIVE

RICARDO
Miguel's Burial

MOSTLY I didn't understand what was going on or what was wanted of me. I felt as though I were living between something that was dying and something not yet born, without much to steady me. I was flying blind. All I knew was that I needed to hold on to this strangeness or I would be overcome by my inner vertigo. I had to hang on. And for the next few days and years I would gradually learn how carefully I was also being held by others. But for now it was a baptism, a fire-and-drowning baptism, a no-holds-barred immersion into a new world, and — in a way of which I was not aware at the time — into a new family. Anything dead that is coming to life again hurts. I hadn't really known that, and I was hurting.

It was like a baptism by fire, a more-than-bargained-for experience. As I look back at it I see more clearly than before how uprooted I was. No one told me that following a passionate commitment would be so much like losing one's self. I had expected something like "coming home," with a wonderful integration of heart and action, of longing and finding. But here I was sitting in a jeep in the San Felipe section of old Panama waiting for my three new friends to return. I had just arrived in the Republic of Panama and felt lost, not simply because I was in unfamiliar surroundings, but more importantly because so much that was familiar, so much that mattered to me, had been left behind. This disorientation and grief was my baptism, my rebirth into a new reality.

I am a priest in the Episcopal Church, a *gringo* in Latin America, very recently having lived and worked in Princeton, New Jersey, a place of wealth and education that could hardly be more distant from the streets of San Felipe, Panama City. I, Ricardo, as I am called here, have begun to be immersed into a new culture and among new friends. Though it is not clear just yet who I will become, I know painfully what I have left behind. But I am moving too fast in this story, so first let me tell you about my new friends: Chan, Florenzio, and Ismael. Gentle Chan, quiet and steady, and godfather to Miguelito, a twelve-year-old boy who had just died. Florenzio, impulsive but good natured, willing to do almost anything for his friends, relative of Ismael. Ismael, a young man, hard to know very well, with the appearance of someone who is always sad, father of the boy who had died.

These friends have just emerged from the Health Ministry located in an old French-style wooden building on the plaza San Felipe. It was almost mid-day and the streets of this densely populated *barrio* were filled with people, filled with the noise of street merchants and hustlers, of children and sidewalk domino players. The *plaza* was full of color and passion as thick as the tropical heat blanketing the *barrio* and rich with the smell of local food. It was heavy too with fumes from the ever-present *chivas,* the brightly col-

The chiva

ored buses that move about the City with impunity as lords of the street. Painted with scenes of romantic passion and of the icons of impassioned religion, these buses wore on the windows and doors the names of *señoritas* and saints, and the faces of the heroes of popular culture.

This is the old part of the City, built before the turn of the century by the French who had dreamed of constructing the canal across the Panamanian isthmus. But greed, arrogance, and deceit defeated them, as these things in new ways continue to defeat the poor of this neighborhood. What remains of the French legacy is this old *barrio*, full of crusty charm, of rusted wrought iron balconies and open plazas, and of crowded wooden tenements waiting for the next fire. Full of energy and faded charm, San Felipe vibrates with the soul of urban Panama, with a rich mixture of West Indian and Latin colors and cultures.

My friends and I were somewhat out of our element, in

an unfamiliar setting none of us understood very well. They were *campesinos,* country folk, working through as best they could the bureaucracy of the Ministry of Health, trying to obtain the body of a young boy who had died two days ago at Hospital Santo Tomás. I was a newly arrived North American priest trying to be of help. For the moment we were all stymied, unable to figure out what to do next, as we had just failed to obtain the necessary documents needed to obtain the body of young Miguelito.

This story began for me a day ago when I had celebrated my first Eucharist in Monte Claro. After the *misa* I was approached by Cristino Sánchez — Don Tino — the mayor of the village. He wanted to know if I could help a family in the community. A twelve-year-old son of the Ramos family had died in the government hospital the day before. Since the family had few resources, help was needed to obtain the body and bring it back to Monte Claro for burial. Miguel died, I was told, because of heart problems caused by infant malnutrition.

Early this morning I met Ismael, Miguelito's father, and two other men from Monte Claro, one being Miguel's *padrino* (godfather). Together — Ismael, Florenzio, Chan, and I — we spent the next two days trying to gain permission to pick up the boy's body. In office after office, with form after form, we waded through the frustration and anger of trying to obtain the necessary permissions. As I waited alone out on the street I began to realize how vulnerable and powerless the poor are. In subtle and not so subtle ways these men were treated as if their concerns were of no importance. The belief seemed to be that the poor have no feelings. They do not grieve. They are used to accepting whatever comes their way, quietly and passively. At least that appeared to be the prevailing attitude of official after official. Others can experience the frustrations of bureaucratic insensitivity and rigidity, but my friends come to it all with no resources: no money, no information, no *palanca* (clout).

I was doing the best I could. My Spanish was adequate but my friends talked with a different accent, and with a kind of Spanish characteristic of the *campo*. I could get only half of it as my ear tried to retune itself. So I missed a lot, and felt more and more isolated and powerless.

At the end of this first day together we returned to Monte Claro, all of us exhausted. I agreed to meet my friends there early the next morning. I said good-bye to Ismael who was very tearful. His two friends who had cared for him in remarkably gentle ways throughout the day walked back with him into the interior of the village. He was grieving as much for his son as for the humiliation he had faced in the City. Grief was close to anger for him. He knew also that his two *compadres* had lost much needed pay by being with him today. But it was clear to Chan and Flores that this loss didn't matter as much as being there for their friend. What are families and *padrinos* for if not for this? So they lived out their loyalty quietly and with strength.

Early the next morning I picked them up and drove to Tocumen, a settlement near the airport about twenty kilometers from the City. Here we gathered in a small house where Ismael and a friend built a box for Miguelito, a coffin made of rough-hewn planks and lined with white cotton fabric bought the day before. It seemed as though many of the people in the house were *familiares*, relatives of some sort of Ismael's. Later we were fed small tamales and coffee and sent on our way back to Santo Tomás to pick up the remaining papers.

It was not to be that easy! We found that we needed two more documents and $15 before we would have access to Miguel's body. Fifteen dollars is two day's pay for Ismael! But within a couple of hours we had both money and papers.

Florenzio, the *padrino,* Miguel's grandmother, and I went to the morgue with Ismael. It was up to us to prepare the body. We carried the rough box from the jeep, as curious bystanders gathered on the street to see what was going to happen. We found Miguelito laid out, naked on a small table in a stark and cold room. We dressed him with a new shirt and trousers from Machetazo, the popular discount department store on Avenida Central. We sprinkled him with cheap cologne and laid him carefully in the box. The grandmother wept quietly in the corner of the room. Ismael, silent, was too tired to feel much; the two day's struggle had worn him thin of heart and feeling. We prayed together, and I blessed the body, asking God to be with Miguelito on his new journey. There was both gentleness and sadness about it all. Miguel seemed so fragile and small.

We carried him back to the jeep for the ride to Monte Claro. The last mile or so after entering the village the trail was wet and muddy, so we were forced to walk the rest of the way. Florenzio and Chan carried the body up and down the muddy path as I followed with Ismael and his mother. We soon came to the house where the funeral Mass would be celebrated. About forty *familiares* and friends had come, crowding into the small *ranchito* of bamboo and palm. The casket was in the middle of an open space, and a small table was prepared next to it for the altar. The smell of heliotrope filled the room from the glass of flowers placed near a faded picture of the *corazón sagrado de Jesús* and beside a candle.

How does one speak of hope in this situation? How can

the Good News of the reign of God be shared in ways that do not minimize the web of grief, suffering, and powerlessness of which the death of this young boy was a reminder?

We prayed. I spoke of the God who weeps, of the One who loves not from a safe distance, but who comes among us touched by our tears, wounded by our brokenness, but whose nearness and love brings healing and hope within our grief. We reminded one another that in the midst of what we do not understand there is a love that will not let us go, a love from God that nothing, not even suffering or death, can destroy. The tenderness and care of Ismael's friends were signs of this love. The gathering and Eucharist were also signs. We shared communion, all of us: men, women, children, young and old. I did not learn until afterward that children do not usually receive. But they had come gladly and with need, and so were fed. Afterward I knelt beside the weeping father, unable to do or say anything but simply to be at his side.

Being present! So much of what I've learned these last two days has to do with the power of being present to those in need. That's what the people of Monte Claro taught me. Love takes many forms, but when all has been exhausted, simply remaining, standing with people in their need is the deepest gift we can offer. Here we call it *solidaridad*, a word that refers to more than proximity. Being present is participation in the joy and suffering of a people, a participation without immunity, a "being with" not from a safe distance but in ways that weave and entangle us. *Solidaridad*. Presence. Becoming flesh with each other.

I had many thoughts as I returned to the City. Most of all I thought that in a world where effectiveness is so often measured by the capacity to effect change or by the ability to realize accomplishments, here today were people who seldom could change anything, but who knew the power of being with each other for love and loyalty's sake. There had been an experience of healing and grace for them as well as for me. That, in a way, was Miguelito's last gift to us.

I crossed the Puente de las Américas and could see the full moon hanging over the bay. There was unspeakable beauty about it. It shown too over Ismael's house, and Chan's and Florenzio's. Did they see it? Are they able to let the experience of beauty speak with at least as much clarity and power as today's time of grief?

Down Avenida de los Mártires I drove, where fruit vendors sell papaya and melons into the night, and street women along Calle Jota invite young men and old to come inside and forget the oppressiveness of the tropical night for a while. I remembered the simple burial ground on the outskirts of Monte Claro where we buried Miguel. The men dripped under the heat and thickness of the afternoon as they dug the grave for the young boy. Wet *guayabera* shirts clung to their backs as they filled in the hole. One by one they shoveled the dirt, everyone taking a turn. I offered prayers and commended Miguel and us to God's loving care: *polvo a polvo,* dust to dust . . . *en esperanza segura y cierta . . . que su alma . . . descansa en paz.*

The heat and the wetness were a part of my ongoing baptism. It was not the same baptism as that of Ismael and his family. I could not begin to enter that experience. But my own passage was that of stranger becoming friend, of foreigner becoming the community's pastor and companion. I had been with the people of Monte Claro sharing something of their powerlessness. I had been with them not as one who had the answers, as one who could provide solutions or help in the bitter dealings with power and bureaucracy. I couldn't even exert *palanca*, influence enough to grease the wheels of justice. They knew about my helplessness, about my own confusion and lostness. Respecting my embarrassment at times, concerned for my role as priest, gentling me in fumblings and confusions they cared for me, even when they had more than enough to do to care for each other.

Un molino la vida nos tritura con dolor, we often sing at the Eucharist. "Life like a mill grinds us painfully." I've seen Señora Valeria grind *maíz* on her grinding stone, and I understand the image. But the song continues: *Somos trigo del mismo sembrador...Dios nos hace Eucaristía en el amor.* "We are wheat from the same sower...God in love makes us Eucharist." So the harsh milling can be life-giving after all.

A stranger. Baptized anew. Milled grain. *Solidaridad.* Hurting as dying becomes new life. What remains with me is the sweet smell of heliotrope, the smell of death, but of more: the sweet reminder of life that will not stop, that will not be beat down. What I was beginning to smell was the soft, fecund aroma of the *solidaridad* that is stronger than death.

I, baptized Ricardo, *gringo* priest among the people of Monte Claro, Panama...I have begun a new journey. Immersed into a reality beyond my control, I am learning and growing. But I am not alone on this journey and this growing. I have friends now. All of us together are learning of what a well-known refrain says: *No hay camino, se hace el camino por caminar.* For this journey "there is no road; the road is made by walking," and we have done a lot of walking together these past two days!

SIX

EL MERCADO
The Market

In the narrow passage
where scattered remains
of banana and papaya
smell sweet
and mingled with the decay
of the week's sweat
for a *balboa* or two,

a mother's breast
feeds a child
with a fly on his cheek,

and the small girl
who carries a brother
on her back
begins
a long line
of burdens
which one day
will hardly be distinguishable
from herself,

she cautiously looks
above her
still flame in her eyes,
fire which one day
will glaze over
to lighten the heaviness,

eyes which now
remain silent,
the better
to weep later,

and moves into the crowd
of flesh and heat
hardly distinguishable
from herself.

SEVEN

ISMAEL
La Junta

IT was late in the afternoon when Padre, Bethy, and I climbed the last hill leading to the Casa Comunal, the place we would gather for our meeting. Though the sun was at the horizon, I could still feel the day's heat rising from the powder-dry earth, heat that clung without mercy to the heavy and humid air. It was the dry season, and very hot. But as we climbed I could feel across the wetness of my skin the first touch of the late afternoon breeze.

Almost as if by signal the cicadas began singing. It was more like a cry than a song. Our people believe that cicadas weep for the passion of Jesus. Each year they begin their song in the Lenten season and cry each night through Holy Week as a sign of sorrow for the sufferings of Jesus. Often we have to compete with the noise, Padre sometimes having to stop the *misa* for a moment to wait for their sound to die away.

Down the path a bit I could see Chan waiting for us, watching with his broad, ever-present smile. His smile always amazes me, for I know that often there is little for him to be glad about. Nevertheless he is full of life and of God, and so it is hard to be sad around him. Down deep inside him there is an unshakable joy and humor, as deceptive of reality as is his youthful look. "I'm older than you think," he always says." And it's true. But we tease him about it a lot. "Old man with a child's face!," we always call him.

"Buenas tardes," I shouted before we had arrived to where he was. *"Buenas,"* he shouted back and waved the palm branch he'd been using to clean the Casa Comunal. *"¿Cómo estás, hermano?"* we asked. *"¡Ay! aquí regular,"* he responded in his noncommittal way.

Commitment is hard around here. Commitments depend on reliability, and this in turn rests on hope. Hope — *esperanza* — is what we have only in short supply here. So our tendency is to stand around on the edge of life, waiting to see what will happen. Waiting! Though life here is often very hard, there is a lot of time to wait and see. Generations of time.

By now it was dark as one-by-one the members of the Junta appeared, carrying their *taboretes* to sit on. Flores was trying, with a little too much well-meant help from those standing around, to get the propane lantern going. We had instructions in Spanish and English, but they had been written for *gringo* minds. The line of logic here is very different, and we were not at all helped by the printed word. Trial and error would be more useful.

I'm feeling very tired tonight and would rather be somewhere else, perhaps resting at home in my hammock. It's been a hard week. I work in the City taking care of gardens for some rich families. It's good work, but being around those people makes me long for what they have. Sometimes I can't keep from dreaming...." One day...maybe...."

Eugenia, my wife, tells me to stop dreaming about televisions and cars and all that stuff. "You're becoming materialistic like all those *gringos,* and all the Panamanians who want to copy them," she sometimes tells me. She's right, but I can't bear to let her know it. It makes me impatient at times with my people here in Monte Claro. They don't have any ambition. Most of them can hardly read. I often think they are lazy, but maybe it's that they can't allow themselves to hope for much.

I was chosen to be the *guardián mayor* (senior warden) of the new Episcopal congregation here in Monte Claro, named San Isidro Labrador. I am a licensed lay reader in an Episcopal parish in the City. Much of the time I'd rather be there, not here. People there are better educated, have good jobs, and drive cars. When I can I want to move my family from this worn down village to live in the City. But when I think that way I also remember that I am a *campesino,* at least by birth and growing up. My family still lives in the interior of Panama, and I always like to go there. The air is clean and fresh. The *fincas* are rich with corn and rice and beans. And the people are simple and honest. It's a good life, really. So I'm torn so much of the time. Who am I? Where do I really belong? I have the eyes, the mind, and appetite of an *urbano*; but I have the heart and purse of a poor *campesino. "Dios mío, así es la vida."*

The Junta Misionera is a new group organized by Padre Ricardo. It is the first group of leaders chosen for the Episcopal congregation here in Monte Claro. In ways it is all very new, this trying to share leadership and take responsibility for the care of our people. Also new is the understanding that this community is part of the larger Episcopal Church community in Panama — in a partnership rather than a dependency.

A couple of months ago we "elected" our Junta. I say "elected," but we really chose our leaders in a special way. We are not used to doing things in a "democratic" way: that is, asking everyone to vote for what he or she wants. Most of the time we feel that that is not just. Too many people don't get what they want, and it doesn't work. If eight people want one thing, and fifteen want another, we are left with a divided community. So we talk and talk, often for hours and days about some important decision. Sometimes Padre gets very tired or impatient. He tries not to show it, but I know.

After everyone has had their say, at least once or twice, an agreement often happens, something everyone can accept. That's the way the members of the Junta were selected. We talked for a long time about the responsibilities of each member and about the kind of persons we wanted to ask to serve. Then little by little people named names, or some even volunteered. Before we knew it we had two *guardianes* (wardens) and five members, with everyone in agreement. It just happened, and all were pleased. This is the way we do things. Everyone can participate, but all need to agree.

Sometimes, though, it is hard to agree. Often we will choose to wait for a decision. At times we agree before everyone is ready. We end up with a public agreement, but with private disagreements that are buried like *yuca* roots, hidden from view but ready to come up again after the first rain. Sometimes our agreements settle nothing. People are too polite or timid to say what they really think. We are trying to work at being more honest in our meetings, but it's not easy.

Finally Florenzio got the lantern going. We could begin.

It looked as though the Junta meeting was going to be the evening entertainment for a lot of people. In addition to the Junta members, there arrived a number of curious and interested members of the community. The Casa Comunal was full, with people standing around the edges. The Casa is a simple house, with a cement floor and a *techo de paja,* a thatched roof of palm branches. There are no walls, so many people can join us around the outside of the house.

The Casa Comunal

Aurelia, secretary to the Junta, came up the hill with her two children. She is young and *muy bonita,* a mixture of shyness and feminine confidence. I don't mind admitting my heart sings when I see her coming. I think that she is the loveliest woman of the village, but I'm too shy to tell her. I tease her a lot, which I guess is the way I let her know. She is not married, but has two children already. Her man, the father of her children, is not very good to her. He comes and goes and hardly helps her with money or time to care for the children. She lives with her mother and uncle, but they don't have much either. I feel sad for her.

Don Pacífico came too. He is ancient and almost totally blind. But his mind and ears are finely tuned, and he shuffles barefoot, stick in hand, down the path, listening for where the gathering will be. *"Buenas,"* he says as he enters. We all greet him and remind him that this is not a *misa* but a meeting of the Junta. He often gets confused about all this. But he seemed pleased to be in on tonight's gathering.

We are still learning how to function as a committee. Each of us lacks certain basic skills and experience, but each person also comes with some rich gifts. Aurelia is very faithful, hardly ever missing a meeting. Mari is very bright and has a lot of good ideas. Victor has a lot of energy, but often talks too much. Chan is quiet, but very practical. Catalino is not very dependable, but when he is around his energy and enthusiasm are contagious, and he often helps us get beyond our discouragements. We have a lot to learn, but everyone has something important to give. If at times we have a hard time getting something done, it is because the people around us are more important than the task. We give more time to each other than we do to our work. But that is something that is rich about us.

Several dogs and Chan's wandering pig, *el chancho,* have joined us. It's all right with me as long as they don't fight. They seem to be attracted by the *convivencia* of the gathering, by the sense of being family together. I guess they think it is good to be around these people tonight.

We began our meeting with a reflection on a story from the Bible. This is done each time we meet so that we can do our work better together as a Christian community, listening to each other at the same time as we try to listen to God. We have learned that there is so much in the Bible for us, so much that describes our life and struggles. I used to think that the Bible was impossible to understand and that I shouldn't try to make sense of it. But with my *compañeros* I'm learning that I can understand, and that I can share my ideas with others too. I read better than most in the community and used to think I knew more. But Padre has helped me see that even Chan, who can't read a letter, can hear God, and can share what he understands with all of us.

I think that the Bible speaks to us best when we hear it through each other's eyes and ears. And so we always begin by reading. One person reads and then each person shares what he or she has heard. Padre and Bethy help us to ask questions about our life in Monte Claro and encourage us to bring these questions to the biblical story. We see often how the people with whom Jesus lived shared so many of the experiences we do and how Jesus had a special concern for the poor and the powerless, for people just like us. Knowing this helps us to feel important in the eyes of Jesus. But we are also learning that Jesus doesn't do things for us like a great *patrón*. No, he helps us to become a community, to become people who care for each other, who stand with each other in good times and in times when we suffer.

Tonight's reading was a reading from St. Paul. He wrote about how Christian community was like a body: it was something that had many parts and many functions, but whose parts are all needed to work together for God's will. I may not have it all just right. But this is how I remember it.

We talked about how the little church in Monte Claro is like a body. It has a head and arms and legs. It has eyes and ears, hands and heart, feet and mouth. All the parts are there, and all are important. If one gets sick, the whole body hurts. We so often think of the church as a group of individuals who come to Mass, say their prayers, light a candle, and then go home. We were learning to see that Jesus is among us as the head of the body, the one who forms us into a community in which everyone is important.

Padre asked us to think about this image of the body. With what part of the body did we most identify? What part we would like to be? Or what part do we think we are? Some said they were hands because they liked to work on projects. Some said they were eyes and ears because people came to them to share their troubles and joys. Some were like the heart because they felt deeply for the struggles of their friends. Two young boys said they were like feet because Padre always sends them running up and down the hills to tell people when there is a meeting or a *misa*. We all discovered a part of the body we thought we were like.

Then Padre and Bethy helped us look at the community, to see which parts of the community, which parts of the body we were looking down on, which parts we didn't think were important. We talked about things that wound the body, that make it sick and not work very well. We talked about which parts of the body needed special care because they are weak.

At first I felt bad because I identified myself with the head. I am smart and I have more education than most people in Monte Claro. I often think I am better than others because of my education. But now I see that other parts of the body are important too. I see better that if the community is like a body, we do need each other. Everyone is poorer, everyone is weaker when other parts are not cared for or are not seen to be valuable. It's a hard thing to learn, but I am learning.

Padre closed by saying that we are not just any body, we are the body of Christ in Monte Claro. I've always thought of Christ's body as being on the crucifix in the church, or being like a miracle in the bread and wine we receive in the *misa*. But this was new, and it filled my head to almost bursting. We the church, the small community of Christians in Monte Claro, are the body of Jesus. And when we abandon each other, when we look out only for our own needs, we break the body, we wound it all over again. Jesus must hurt a lot in Monte Claro. We have so far to go to be a strong and healthy body.

It was after 9:30 P.M. when we finished that night. By then the dogs had wandered off. The children were sound asleep in laps or at nursing breasts. The Junta had done good work, and we knew it. I felt deep joy at being able to be a part of it all, slow and painful as it was at times.

Victor, the junior warden, offered a closing prayer. Old blind Don Pacífico had already gone. I hadn't heard him leave. I wonder how he found his way home in the dark, but then I remembered it was always dark for him.

Before we ended our meeting we sang a song. Padre Ricardo always brings his guitar for someone to play. We sang one of my favorite songs:

> *Junto a tí al caer de la tarde,*
> *y cansado de nuestro labor,*
> *te ofrecemos con todos los hombres,*
> *el trabajo, el descanso, el amor.*

> Together with you at the close of the day,
> and tired from our labor,
> we all offer you together
> our work, our rest, and our love.

"Qué le vaya bien," we said at our leaving. *"Vaya... vaya'* we heard in the distance as we walked down the road with Padre and Bethy to find their jeep. The cicadas were quiet now. Only the bright sliver of a new moon was left in the clear dark sky to accompany us as we walked. *Poco a poco,* I thought. Change happens slowly here, but something is beginning to happen. At least in me.

EIGHT

VALERIA
Time and Blessing

I HAVE been down all morning at the *quebrada* where the stream is, where I do my washing and bathing and take the children to play. It's a long walk from my house, but usually I don't mind. On the way I pass the *ranchos* of many of my friends and have the opportunity to visit with them and get caught up on the news of their lives.

I almost always take the children with me. They are not my children, really. Carlito and María belong to Aurelia, my daughter. Luis is the son of my niece, who is not able to care for him, and so he lives with me. Here I am, a grandmother, and each day I'm in charge of three children all under seven years of age!

My daughter, Aurelia, is a good mother and loves to be with her children. But she has to work in the City as often as possible. She brings in the only outside income we have as a family, and so works a lot, ironing clothes for a woman in the wealthy *barrio* of El Dorado.

When we are down at the *quebrada* the children play while I work. They love to swim in the stream, shouting and splashing, making up games with water and mud, probably as children do all over the world. I always have them play downstream so that I can have some clean water in which to wash and bathe.

Washing is hard work, and I do it for seven people. But I sing while I wash and the time goes fast. I try to make good use of all my time, for I feel that every day, every minute is a gift from God, and I must receive it and hold it carefully like I did precious Carlito when he was only a few days old. When I wake each morning I always say, *Gracias a Dios por darme otro día.* "Thank you my God for giving me another day."

Time is a special thing for me. My past is full of hard memories, of troubles and struggles too many to name. And my future: what can I say? I try not to count on it too much. The future for me is more like a part of a circle, like the repetition of things from the past. Nothing new much happens for me. So I stay away from the future, except to think about when to plant my garden or when to celebrate the saint days, the birthdays of members of my family.

But the present? I have learned to hold it and cherish it and to receive whatever God gives me day by day. It's better that way, and for me, more gentle. I deal only with what is present, and enjoy surprises that come unannounced, or endure as quietly as I can unbidden pain. I give myself to my family and to my care for them, and I weep when I must. But basically I take one day at a time. And mostly I'm a happy and content woman, not fretting much over what was or won't be.

I'm a lot like my friend, my *comadre* Marcelina. She lives not too far from me, and we like to spend a lot of time together. When times are hard she holds me, and I hold her. We are like sisters, although we have known each other for only ten years or so. She is godmother to my Anna.

Marcelina and I work together when we can. Sometimes we cook or prepare chickens for sale. We work together often at the clothing sale we have every two months in the community. Bethy and Padre bring us used clothes they gather in the City. Marcelina and I, often with the help of other women of the village, sort and price the clothes. We sell them for just a few *centavos* so that people can have the dignity of paying for what they own. All the money we receive goes into the treasury of the women's group for projects in the community. Right now we are saving money to help finish the school.

It is good to have a friend like Marcelina, someone I can trust, who I can talk with. Sometimes I feel so alone because I have no family with me. I have my own children and my brother, of course. But I miss the rest of my family, my parents and my cousins and *padrinos*. At times I feel so cut off from my past, from the countryside where I grew up, from the rich collection of *familiares* that were always so much a part of my childhood, but now who are scattered or dead. But in my aloneness I have discovered my friend Marcelina, and I have come to see each moment of time with her as something to be held and treasured. Little by little, with the help of friends like Marcelina, I have come to find joy in my days, simple as they are.

We sing a song during the *misa* when Padre brings his guitar. The song talks about being glad for each day, receiving it as a special gift, and blessing God for life given each new morning. It is one of my favorite songs, and it says:

Demos gracias al Señor, demos gracias...
En la mañana que se levanta el día canta,
y yo canto al Creador...

Let us give thanks to the Lord, let us give thanks...
In the dawning of the morning the day sings,
and I too sing to the Creator...

I try to find God's blessing in everything, because I believe everything is holy.

Speaking of everything being holy, I remember several weeks ago when Padre Ricardo visited my family, and I was made aware again of how sacred the little things of my life are. Padre's visit was a special event for us, because no priest had ever visited us before. I made sure we were all there to greet Padre. My brother, Juan, was there, and sober, *gracias a Dios*. My two daughters were there also, along with all their children. And even my cousin Fito came, from where he lives down by the *quebrada;* he had never met Padre. So we were a grand family that day, and I was proud.

We had worked all morning cleaning up the *patio*. We are very poor and don't have much, but what we have can be made to look lovely, and it was. Aurelia cooked some corn cakes for us to eat. And I made some *chichemi,* a drink with warm milk, rice or corn, and raw sugar.

We were all ready before Padre came up the path, and were a bit nervous too; at least I was. My daughters were giggling like two overexcited hens, but I knew it was because they were anxious. Would Padre like us? Would he like our house and *patio?* Would he eat what we cooked?

Everyone had put on his or her best clothes. I told Juan in the morning that he had to go down to the stream and bathe. I treat him like my son sometimes, even though he is ten years older than me. But he needs some mothering from time to time.

"Hola," cried Padre as he came up the hill to the house. *"Buenas tardes, amigos. ¡Cómo están todos?"* We all greeted him with our smiles, but for a moment no one said anything. We were still nervous. Then Juan started laughing. *"Ay,* Padre, the cat has all the tongues of my family; it's the first time ever, I'm sure," he said.

Padre went around the patio, with its clay hardened floor, greeting everyone by name, taking each one's hand. My youngest daughter, Anna, was very shy and was hardly able to greet Padre. The small children were all giggles. But finally everyone was greeted. My cousin, Fito, didn't respond much at first. He is very old and deaf and sometimes doesn't understand what's going on. But once he gets going, *¡caramba!* he's impossible to stop.

My own heart was racing, but inside I was very glad when Padre come up to give me a hug. Strong and warm are his *abrazos.* The day too gave its embrace. It was one of those partly overcast Panamanian afternoons, hot and humid, but with relief from the sun. It hadn't rained yet that afternoon, so the mud wasn't a problem. It was a day kissed by the angels, I thought.

My house is really a compound of *ranchos,* of small houses built around a dirt patio, made with bamboo sticks and palm, with *techos de paja,* roofs of palm branches. In one *rancho* Aurelia and the children sleep. One is for cooking. The big one is our living room where we gather at the end of each day. It is an open *rancho* without walls. Another small *rancho* is for my brother. And still another, for me. My husband has been dead for many years, so I sleep alone.

As I remember it didn't take long for the conversation to

begin. Usually we *campesinos* don't talk freely with strangers or with people we don't know well. Padre is new to our community, but already I like him and he is easy to talk with.

Well, we told stories of our family, of where we came from, and of how long we had been in Monte Claro. *Dios mío*, it's been over ten years now! We moved here several years after my husband had died, having lived in the province of Los Santos in the interior of Panama. I was left to live with the family of my *marido*, my husband, and they never did like me. So life was very hard. My brother suggested we come to Monte Claro, where we had a cousin. Land was free for the settling on it. And we thought that being near the City would mean more work for us. So we left everything and everyone and came, leaving the area my family had lived

Panamanian pottery based on Precolumbian designs

in for many generations. But what could I do? I was alone and with people who didn't want me.

We talked too about the community. Poor *Padrecito* — he got an earful. I don't like complaining about the community or talking behind people's backs. I'd rather say something directly to a person I'm bothered with, or keep silent. But the rest of my family is different. They have opinions on everything. *Ay, Dios,* they shared with Padre Ricardo all their thoughts. Thoughts about the local government and its failed promises to Monte Claro. Thoughts about the new school, and how it should have been built somewhere else, more central in the community. Thoughts about the Junta Comunal, its good ideas and bad. Thoughts about the new Episcopal congregation in Monte Claro, and about why it's a good thing "even though we don't often come." Padre listened well, but at times seemed not to get what was being said. I think he was quite exhausted after an hour or so.

We talked about family problems too. Sometimes we get upset with each other about little things. I get upset about big things too, like Juan's drinking, or about how little money we have. And I wish Aurelia would help me more with the children. We talked about the news that my daughter Anita is pregnant again. We talked about the corn and rice that was just planted. We talked about the chicken project the women have organized, about which the men are very skeptical. We talked about who is ill and who has recovered recently in the community. The children shared their excitement about the opening soon of the new school. We talked about the weather, always about the weather! And Padre shared some of his hopes for the work of the church here in Monte Claro.

I was amazed at how freely everyone shared thoughts. It's

good to be able to talk like this, and we usually have so little opportunity or take time to do so. I even learned some new things about my family.

Later in the afternoon we had coffee together from beans we grow on our *finca*. We gave Padre the *chichemi,* which he liked very much. I didn't have enough milk or sugar to make some for everyone, but they understood. Padre was our special guest. Then Aurelia, proud as the rising sun, brought out her corn cakes and we had a real *fiesta*.

By the time the sun had gone down almost below the tip of the mountains near the ocean, the time most of the men start coming home, the afternoon breezes, the *sereno,* had begun. Padre, getting up to leave, asked if he could bless the family. I hoped he would ask, so I had a pot of water ready for him. I like to have holy water on hand to sprinkle on the children to keep them well and safe, to protect them from the *aires,* the winds and spirits that blow near the *quebradas* and sometime make people sick. One time I even sprinkled some on my brother, Juan, when he was sleeping off a hard night of drinking. *¡Carajo!* I was so frustrated with him, I didn't know what to do. So I prayed to God for help and secretly sprinkled him. To this day he doesn't know I did it. He would call me a foolish old woman if he found out.

Padre took the water and prayed a beautiful prayer over it. He offered thanksgiving to God for the gift of water, remembering how richly water touches our lives: water for crops and food, for coffee and *chicha,* for cleansing and healing, for baptism and for being reminded of God's love.

He prayed for protection for us from the water, prayed that it would be our friend and not our foe. At times water swells the streams of the *quebradas,* filling them to the point of danger. The long rainy season brings with it a season of sickness for those of us who live on the clay hillsides of Panama, exposed to the endless storms. He prayed too for clear, drinkable water for the community, for safe water that we have yet to obtain.

In our prayer together we tried to name everything. We blessed the water so that we would be reminded better of God's presence and love among us. We blessed the water so that we would be more able to find God both in what is given to us, as well as in what is taken away, to know God's presence in times both wet and dry.

Then I led Padre around our patio. I wanted God to bless all of our home, everything and everyone in it. Who knows how long it will be before Padre comes to see us again? I won't let him go without a blessing.

So we went all around the yard, *rancho* by *rancho,* place by place. Padre prayed, I sprinkled water. Before we finished almost everything we had talked about that afternoon was wet with God's blessing. I knew that this thirsty world of ours needed God's presence and blessing. Dripping with holiness, my harsh and lovely world was blessed, the ugly with the beautiful, the gentle with the hostile, the fearful with what was beginning to be filled with hope.

Beds, chickens, pots and pans, children, pregnant women, deaf old men, plans and discouragements, meanness and love: all were wet with this blessing, all were woven together now with a deeper awareness of God's presence and care for us all. Nothing was left unbaptized that afternoon. Nothing was left outside the *patio* of God's care and presence. For me it was all holy.

¡Ay, Dios mío! Padre never knew what had happened to him, visiting the house of this crazy old woman! But I could tell by his eyes and by his stillness that he too had been

blessed by God. He was glad to have been with us, glad to have shared a sacred moment of our time.

Each time now that I go down to the *quebrada* to wash or bathe, I look carefully at the water. I take time to see it, to touch it, and to taste its coolness on my tongue. I remember Padre's visit to our family and I give thanks to God. I remember holy water being sprinkled over everything that matters to me. I remember and am glad. And when I feel sorry for myself, sorry for being so poor, sorry for being hungry, sorry for the children when they are sick and I can't do much for them, sorry when my brother is drunk and can't work the fields as we need him to: when I start feeling sorry like this I remember the water and the blessing. And I remember that I, Doña Valeria, did something that day: I remembered what was important in my family's life, and I asked God to bless it.

Life is still hard for us. Aurelia still goes off to the City to find work. Juan is still hard to depend on. The children are as demanding as they are dear to me. And the table remains bare much of the time. But life no longer seems so repetitive. I see new things happening to me and to my community. Maybe someday my past won't seem so much like a mountain of suffering. Maybe the future will offer more and more possibilities for change, for what can be new. And most of all maybe my present, my moments and my days can be filled with blessing, with reminders of the love and care that surround me and my people, the love and care we all touched that day when my house was blessed.

NINE

FLORENZIO
Viacrucis

I'M used to it, but *¡Ay!* the sun is brutal today. I stand out in the sun almost every day, swinging the machete, earning my bit of bread. But for some reason the brightness and heat this afternoon are almost too much for me. Today is Holy Friday, the day of crucifixion. We are here, almost all of us from Monte Claro, walking in procession through the community on the Way of the Cross, recalling the fourteen stories of Jesus' passage through the streets of Jerusalem to Calvary. We do this each year, house to house. And as we process we sing, *"Te adoramos, O Cristo, y te bendecimos. . . . "* "We adore you, O Christ, and we bless you. . . . "

Just now we are trying to gather into Señora Valeria's newly built *rancho*. This house is a story in itself; maybe I can tell it later. But here we are, almost fifty last I counted. *"Porque con tu santa cruz has redimido al mundo. . . . "* "Because by your holy cross you have redeemed the world. . . . " Everyone is singing now, and for me it's both beautiful and *un poco triste*, a bit sad. It is beautiful because we don't often sing together, and our voices express so much of our life and our longings. Today this is very beautiful. But in a way it is sad too: not so much for the voices, but for the day. *Viernes Santo,* Holy Friday is a solemn day for us. We think a lot about Jesus dying on the cross. In all of our houses hangs a crucifix. We can understand his sufferings and being rejected, because we suffer too. We are an abandoned people. The crosses of our suffering in this community are too many to count. And so we sing as people who know the music by heart.

We sing as people who do not have enough to eat, as those whose children are constantly threatened with malnutrition and disease. We sing as people without a voice, to whom no one listens, neither the government, nor employers, nor — until recently — the church. We are a people who try to live off the land, but with land too poor to support us. We are a people, most of us, who can't read or write. And our children are in danger of growing up the same way, because our little ones have no school they can attend. We sing as a people burdened by our powerlessness, our inability to change our life for the better. We are a people who know daily the harsh blows of a unjust world. Yes, we know the music of the cross all too well.

Ricardo, our priest here in Monte Claro, says that where he comes from people call this day Good Friday. I asked him once, "Why do some people call this day 'good'?" For me it's a sad day, totally sad. Jesus came to love people, and they killed him. He came to teach them about God and they turned against him. The more he loved and taught, the fewer friends he had. At least that is the way it seems to me. But Ricardo said, "Listen to the words you are singing: 'Because by your holy cross you have redeemed the world.' Isn't this good news? Isn't there something about the death and res-

urrection of Jesus that says to us there is nothing in this life, even in our most bitter troubles, that cannot be touched by the redeeming love of God?" This Lent Ricardo has been trying to help us see some new things about being people of an Easter faith. Our churches are full on Good Friday, but almost empty on Easter Day. "We know a lot about crosses," says Padre, "but we have a hard time knowing much about resurrections." And that's true, I think.

The religion many of us grew up with focused on the suffering Jesus, on Jesus of the cross. The history of Latin America for the majority of its people, and our history here in Monte Claro, has been one of continuous suffering and oppression. It is easier for us to understand Jesus' sufferings than it is to see how these sufferings are overcome in the resurrection. The resurrection of Jesus, and the hope it brings, still seem far away from our experience.

After reading the story of one of the stations of the cross and offering some prayers, we move on. *"Te adoramos, O Cristo, y te bendecimos...."* we sing as we move on to Don Tino's house. More people are following now. The afternoon procession has been going on a half hour or so, and we have three hours left to go. At each house we pick up more people. Children, old men, stray dogs, and some wandering chickens: everyone follows. Across the hills from house to house the procession moves like a great fiesta. I lead with the cross. Young and beautiful Mariana carries the incense. Padre and Don Tino follow. And spread out in a long line are the pilgrims of Monte Claro. Some pilgrims! At times they seem like a crowd at a soccer match. Señora Marcelina tells the young people to follow more quietly.

Before the late afternoon breezes come we will have visited almost every house in the village. The sky is cloudless, so from time to time we have to stop under a tree to cool off in the shade. Our community is scattered on several hillsides. Corn fields and tropical growth cover the land. The dusty pathways wander up and down the hills and across stream beds almost dry now for lack of rain. In my mind I try to picture how it was for Jesus, going up and down the hills, tired and hungry. People shouting at him, throwing things. And his cross: *muy pesado,* very heavy. *¡Dios mío!* I can't imagine how he did it.

We stop at each house where someone reads one of the stories about Jesus and his journey through Jerusalem, carrying his cross. Then we talk about what this part of the story means to us here in Monte Claro. Padre blesses the house, sprinkles holy water all around, and we sing again: *"Porque con tu santa cruz has redimido al mundo. . . . "*

In front of Victor's house we read the story of Simon of Cyrene, the man compelled to help Jesus carry his cross. Ramón said that he thought Simon was a foreigner, and according to our tradition a black man like the *antillanos* of Panama. He was a *campesino,* too, who had just come into Jerusalem from the countryside. In this way he was like one of us.

It's curious, someone said, that one of the less fortunate persons in the crowd was asked to help Jesus. And he seemed to do it willingly.

Señora Mili, who hardly ever says anything, said that she thought what was most important in our community was not simply to point out where needs are, but to begin to respond with concrete action. "Simon did something to help," she said. "Jesus is hidden all over our community in the lives of the most needy, among those who carry the heaviest burdens of life. Even though we all are poor like Simon, we can help carry some of these crosses."

I said earlier that I felt honored to be chosen to carry the cross today. It's the first time I have ever done this. But more important is what comes from my story. You see, I have a lot of problems. In some ways I have more good things in my life than others have around here. I am one of the first residents of the community and live on one of the best hills of Monte Claro, with good land and a beautiful view of the whole community. I am married and have been for over twenty-five-years, *gracias a Dios.*

My *señora* is a good woman, though we have had a lot of problems together. I have one of the best jobs in the community, working under contract with a group of men that cuts grass for the Canal area and for U.S. military bases. We swing machetes all day long. But my pay is good, and I have some pension and health benefits, something few men have. So I should be happy, right? I should be thankful to God for all of these blessings. I should be a man of honor and respect in the village. But most of the time I am not. I drink a lot.

Last year, after talking with Ricardo, I had almost half a year with very little drinking. My wife was happy, and I was too. I was able to work a lot in the community, helping to build the school and the new chapel. But then I had problems with my back. I had to stop working for a while, lost my job temporarily, and became very discouraged. My old problem has returned, even though I pray to God to help me not to drink. It's my burden, and it is a heavy one for me and my family.

I remember a year ago, when Ricardo asked me if I would like to carry the cross for the *Viernes Santo* procession, the Way of the Cross. *Con mucho gusto,* I said. "I would be very glad to carry it." But the afternoon of that Friday I came to the procession drunk. Padre said that he was sorry, but he would have to ask someone else. He talked with me a while. I knew I had made him sad. I was angry at myself. But Padre said not to be angry but to come with us and try to listen to the words of hope that we sing and talk about. Even if my head was cloudy with *seco* he wanted me to come. Even if I could not follow very well what was said, I could come with the people and feel the procession through my body as a kind of healing. So I did. Barefoot (for I had lost my shoes) I followed up and down the hills for the next three hours or so. It was very hard for me, but I wanted to do it. Maybe if I suffered a bit Jesus would forgive me. Padre said, "No,

God does not love us more for our self-punishments. God simply loves us, and desires that we be washed and healed and forgiven." Maybe that's true, but I felt better for having cut up my feet for three hours of walking, and for following bare-headed in the hot sun so that God would know I was really sorry.

But this year is different. That is why I feel honored: honored by the community and honored by myself. I am here and I am sober, and I am following Jesus all over these fiery hills.

Many children are with us today. They like the procession and the crowds, and are almost playful. Mariana carries the incense and swings it in every house. Other children help with the readings. Many of our older children can read; most of us adults cannot. So the children feel proud to participate in this way. It is one of the few times their parents get to hear them read.

We move on to Don Goyo and Eulogia's house where we read the story of Veronica, a story that comes from the popular tradition of our people. It is the story of a woman who stepped out from the crowds that day Jesus carried his cross, stepped out with courage and compassion to wipe the face of Jesus. This for me is a strange story, but also very beautiful. Sebastián commented that Veronica must have been very brave to come out from the crowd, to push her way past the soldiers and clean Jesus' sweaty face. I think she probably brought him some water too.

Ricardo asked us, "Where do we find Veronica today?" Tino said he'd seen a lady take the same risk the other day in Panama. This woman stepped out into the street near the university where students were demonstrating to share some fruit with them in the heat of the day. Later some of the *guardia* pushed her back into the crowd, treating her the way I'm sure they would never treat their mothers.

Others in the community said that Jesus is always found among the women, the children, the orphans — found near people who are *los marginados,* those at the edge of life, vulnerable and with little protection. "We have a lot of *los marginados* here in Monte Claro," Señora Marcelina said. "We need to have more Veronicas, women and men of courage who are not afraid to struggle together for a better life. It always seems as though it's only the women who can be counted on to be like Veronica," she said with a flash of passion in her eye. The men grumbled a bit at this idea, but only with a kind playful humor. We knew that a lot of times what she says is true.

Maybe Simon can be the model for our men, just as Veronica is for the women. "Most important," added Bethy, "is the need to be compassionate people, to be a community that notices and then helps clean the suffering faces of our people."

"...porque con tu santa cruz has redimido al mundo." We continue on to the next house.

Ricardo wears his hat, the *sombrero santeño* that the community gave him. He looks very hot and tired in his alb and stole, and the *sombrero* gives him some relief. He looks *puro campesino,* pure peasant just like us, I think to myself. Bethy wears the hat she always wears, her *sombrero vaquero,* her cowboy hat from El Salvador.

Bethy shared a lot with us as we prepared some of the meditations for the Way of the Cross. We talked together about this story, and about how we can discover it within our daily life in Monte Claro. We are walking over our hills today to experience something of the suffering of Jesus on his journey over the hills of his country. Most of us know, however, that it's no good remembering the story of Jesus, or even trying to share in it, without seeing how what is happening in Monte Claro is like what happened in Jesus' time. The connections, Bethy often says, are what matter most. "Jesus is still carrying his cross over the pathways of our village," she says. "Where can we find him? Where can we see him carrying the cross here?"

The more we talked about seeing Jesus in Monte Claro the more we began to notice each other. Bethy says that solidarity comes not only through finding how to walk with Jesus, but also in finding how we can walk with each other. I don't understand all of this, but something is happening inside me. Carrying the cross today, trying to picture Jesus doing the same for us, I find myself more and more where the people are, find myself in the houses of my friends and neighbors, even in some of the houses where I never would have put my feet, being unsure of the welcome. But here I am; here we are: hearing this story, singing these songs, saying these prayers in almost every house, with almost every family of the village.

For some of us this is the first time we have been in the houses of our neighbors. We are seeing these people as ones for whom Jesus carried the cross. We're seeing reminders of suffering and of hope in the eyes and humble dwellings of our people. Sometimes it almost makes me cry. I think of myself, at times, as being the one with the most problems. But now I can see the sufferings and hopes of others more clearly.

Here we are in the house of old Señora Rosita. She is so old she can hardly walk. She lives in her small, run-down *rancho,* with barely anything but the threadbare clothes on her back, and she is offering hospitality to us all. Glasses of *chicha* are being passed around to all of her thirsty friends. I can't imagine where she got the sugar and fruit to make the drink, or where she borrowed enough glasses to share. Clearly she is honored by our visit, probably a first experience like this for her. She cries as she hugs Ricardo when we are about to leave. It is the first time a priest has ever been in her house, she says.

I mentioned earlier that I was going to tell about the blessing of Señora Valeria's new house. Today when we visited her we not only read one of the stations of the cross, but we blessed her house, every corner of it. Six days ago, on the Saturday before Holy Week, her house burnt to the ground, along with almost everything else she owned.

We have the custom in the *campo*, in our rural areas, of burning the brush on the hillsides toward the end of the dry season, just before the coming of the new rains. It helps clear things for planting. Usually in the month of March the air is full of smoke and of little bits of ash raining down like tropical snow. Walking to work each day my hair becomes full of ash. It's in our food, in our beds, our clothes, and our breathing. I don't know why we keep doing it, but each year is the same. For generations it has been the same.

Sometimes the winds come up and the fire gets out of control. That's what happened on the *finca* of Señora Valeria. Her brother was burning the fields and the wind suddenly turned the fire into a wall of terror. Within minutes all was gone. *Gracias a Dios* no one was hurt. Her daughter and grandchildren were away for the afternoon, and only Don Pepe, her brother, was there with her. The fire came so fast that it swept everything away. All the clothes, all of the small *ranchos* where people slept and cooked and ate, all of the food and bedding, gone! I was in the village that afternoon, and as soon as I saw the smoke I ran with some others to see what was happening. When we arrived we saw only patches of black ash where there had been houses and chicken pens, little smudges of loss where once there had been signs of life and of work. Don Pepe was crying a little. I think he was a bit drunk too. Who wouldn't be? Doña Valeria did not show any feelings. She just stood and stared. She never had had much. But now what once she did have she had lost. Baskets and dishes, pots and sheets — gone! Even some of the special things she had done to make her little compound beautiful, some flowers planted, some benches for guests — all gone!

People in the community brought some rice and *yuca* to eat. Some loaned hammocks. Señora Valeria said she wanted to sleep in her own place for the night. The weather was warm and dry, so it would be all right to sleep outside. Other neighbors came to share a few dishes and some clothes for her two grandchildren. Ramón ran around trying to catch the chickens in order to put them in a safe place.

What was most needed was food and some blankets. The community could help with food. Ricardo and Bethy said they would find some sheets and blankets. Why is it that the people who are poorest have to lose the most? Valeria had very little, but now has almost nothing. *"Dios me da lo necesario,"* she says. "God will provide." And she believes this. *"Si Dios quiere"* is always on her lips. "If God wills." Chan and I talked together that day about how we could help her and her brother rebuild.

Two days later, on Monday of Holy Week, Ricardo and Bethy came to the community to celebrate the liturgy of the Palms, since they hadn't been able to come on Sunday.

Padre told me later he was very disappointed about how few men came to the *misa*. There was a good congregation, but mostly of women. Ricardo knows that a lot of drinking begins during holy week. Each year we talk about it in the community, talk about how sad and difficult things become from so much drinking, but still it happens.

After the *misa* Ricardo and Bethy, along with some of the women, came to visit Valeria to see how she was doing. We watched Bethy and Padre coming up the road. "Won't they be surprised," said Don Pepe. And they were. We were just about finished rebuilding Valeria's house. It was a fine house, I thought, and much nicer than she'd had before. We had been working on it since Sunday, finishing it in only two days. Valeria was smiling and proud.

I have seldom seen Ricardo and the others as happy as they were. They were glad to see Valeria and her new house. They were glad to see all of us working so hard for each other. They were glad to see something hopeful in the midst of so much that was hard. Ricardo told us about being disappointed when none of the men were at the *misa*. "But you were all here doing God's work as you worked together for Señora Valeria," he said. "In a way you were celebrating with us by building this house. To work for each other is like praying," he said. "It's *better* than praying," said Bethy, who always puts things more strongly than Padre. And we all laughed.

So today as we blessed Señora Valeria's house, we remembered some very good things that are a part of our community life. This kind of *mutualidad* has not always been true or easy for us. It's not that we don't care about each other. But it is that we have been so caught up in surviving, in taking care of ourselves, that we have a hard time seeing and responding to our *compañeros* when they have needs. We feel that our house is empty, we don't have anything to give. But we're finding that's not true. Maybe this is a little of what Ricardo means when he calls *Viernes Santo* "Good."

The sun still shines down on me like fire. But it doesn't bother me just now. I'm full of the richness of this day, full of new reminders of why there can be hope in Monte Claro. In a way Señora Valeria's new house is a sign of hope for us, a sign that we can overcome our losses. But more than that, it is a sign that we can be together as a community, work together because we belong to each other. Ricardo reminds us that in working together as a community we are coming to know something of the resurrection, we are creating our own stories of hope.

Out of the heat and ashes of Señora Valeria's tragedy has come something new for all of us. I can't quite name it just yet.

TEN

RICARDO
"No, Señor..."

I HAVE been walking along the bay on Avenida Balboa, try-ing to spend some time alone in the midst of a busy week. The late afternoon is caressed with just a touch of breeze, the occasional surprise of late January in Panama. The sky is mostly clear, with a few richly shaped clouds, enough for *dibujos,* as we say here, for pictures you can see in the sky if you have a sufficiently playful imagination. I walk along the wall that separates the modern part of the City from the vastness of the Bay of Panama. Across the bay to the right I can see the colonial part of the City, like a Venetian painting with its baroque towers and imperial buildings golden in the afternoon sun and reflected in the water. On the left are the modern high-rise apartments of Paitilla, a skyline stark and silver. All around me are signs of contrast and contradiction. In front of me are reminders of the prosperity of the 1970s and 1980s, lavish symbols like the ultramodern architecture of the Banco Exterior. It towers above all else seemingly as a guarantor of endless prosperity. In Panama City we have over 150 separate banks, not counting branch offices, for a population of only six hundred thousand, most of whom are too poor to use banks. Nearly every country has a bank here: from Eastern Europe to Chile; from Canada to Japan and Thailand — everyone. Panama is drowning in a "richness" of banks and governments. Such a small country and we have all these banks, along with two separate governments — that of Solís-Palma, and that of Delvalle's government in exile — both claiming legitimacy. We are cursed with blessings.

A young woman from the interior, carrying a baby on her back, approaches me for money. *"Para comer, Señor,"* she said. "So that we can eat." She is young, hardly twenty years old. Her skin is still clear and smooth, unlike the weathered textures of older women from the countryside. She wears the simple, brightly colored dress of her Guayami people. Her hair is deep like the color of a moonless night.

I give her what little change I have, as much from awkwardness as from compassion, and she continues down the street without having made eye contact. Begging is no more fun for her than handing out a small bit of change is for me. Both of us are diminished in this impersonal, humiliating process. But sometimes diminishment is the cost of getting on with things. That's as true for the bankers along Avenida Balboa as it is for this young woman and me. Only I guess the bankers don't yet know it.

The encounter with the *señorita* from the interior has reminded me of how much I have been saying no these days, more than I'm comfortable doing. Probably it is because I don't like it when people say no to me that I try to minimize the nos around me.

I have been saying no a lot to the children who want to wash my car windows at the traffic lights in the City. They are more insistent these days, and so it takes at least two nos: one for the window, the second for the money. I know the game, and they do too. *"Para comer,"* they say, so that perhaps I will get tripped up in the children-hunger-guilt manipulation. Like all manipulations with an edge to them, there is some truth here. So I don't like saying no.

Then there is Miguelito, who comes to wash my whole car. Rain or shine he comes. Because of the current crisis in Panama the price of a car wash has dropped from three dollars to one. Occasionally I say yes, but mostly no. He is often pleading at my door as early as 6:30 A.M.! Sometimes he washes first, asks later, but has found that a bit risky. He's a good washer, but boundaries need to be set. And so I say no to him a lot, even when my car could obviously use some help.

I say no to people who come to the deanery where I live asking for money or food. Rationally I have my reasons. Everyone in our area has been robbed at home at least once lately, one family at knife point. But some reasons are not so rational. Frustration. Powerlessness. Inconvenience. Too many callers these days. Loss of privacy. Even though compelling, these reasons all have a self-serving ring about them.

I remind myself that we have been feeding over a hundred families each week at the cathedral where I serve as dean. And I know that many who come to my house want to get some special attention from the *gringo padre,* hoping to end-run the process as it were. So I say, "No, you need to come by the cathedral office in the morning."

I struggle with the same issues when I leave the City and go to Monte Claro. I said no in Monte Claro to Chepe and his family the other day. That was a hard one for me. I knew they needed the food for which they were asking. And as a church we had been saying that the needs of the people mattered to us. I had food, but I said no.

We have been working with Chepe and his family, and with the whole community, to overcome dependencies where possible, and to find other ways to solve problems than by resorting to patronage or charity.

If we have resources, the community together tries to decide how to use or distribute them. Things given to the community are always given in exchange for something that will build up the people: manual labor, money, volunteer help, involvement in a community project, or whatever. We try to work together as Christian sisters and brothers, not as *patrón* and *peones*.

All this seems perilously close to a guns-or-beans kind of policy: "If you do what we tell you, you get beans; otherwise you are on your own to struggle with the consequences." It also seems close to the way the United States uses food as a tool of foreign policy, as a reward for conforming to U.S. wishes. I think that the difference for us has been the integrity of the community and its attempt to make decisions together about how resources will be shared.

But Chepe came to me as "el Padre," as *patrón*. It had been a long time since he had put much into the life of the community. Now he wanted a favor. I said no, and told him why, but with a heavy heart.

The examples are endless. They come to me in a flood of remembering. I think of the hard nos I have said to my children; to a friend beginning to take advantage of me; to situations where I would have loved to say yes, but for health, sanity, or priority's sake I have needed to say no.

I know all too well that my nos can be signs of avoidance, as well as gestures of care. They can express my "fed-upness" as well as my compassion. For me personally my nos usually come from my head, from my attempt to do "what is reasonable." My yeses come more from my heart, from compassion or a sense of guilt. Motives too get mixed up in all of this. Often my righteous nos (or yeses) can be covers for other dark self-preoccupations. I think I have learned with my children that what I say yes or no to is often less significant than the process — the struggle, really — that is gone through to do the right or honest thing.

Martin Luther once said, "Sin boldly, but believe even more boldly in the love and forgiveness of God." That helps. For my yeses and nos these days need a lot of boldness as well as grace.

Seeing the young Guayami woman and her small child walk away under the shadow of multistoried, international bank buildings increases the moral pressure a bit. The struggle for the heart and reason of it all must take into account the staggering, evil gap between wealth and poverty in the world. Here in Panama, as in most other parts of the world, there is little attempt to smooth over this disparity. In the face of the contradictions between wealth and poverty it is no wonder that consciences become dull or guilt ridden.

There is a lot that is redemptive in this struggle with yes and no. For me the cross of Jesus stands as a sign of this holy struggle. Both yes and no were shouted from Calvary's mountain, by the crucifying authorities as well as by the love of God. God's yes and no survives, and, more than that, empowers us in our struggle to be faithful.

God's yes and no keeps prodding me, keeps drawing me to that day, to that person in whom all our confusions and uncertainties will be gathered, lifted up in the one yes above all others, that bright and blinding yes of Jesus and of the justice and love he came to bring.

Meanwhile I need some help. The woman is gone, but not my awareness of her. She might be amused at the struggle she's caused me. Or maybe not. She might even take me seriously. I turn left to walk up Avenida Frederico Boyd, a broad tree-lined avenue, the gift of more genteel, steady days. A short distance ahead the street is blocked because of a demonstration in front of the Nicaraguan Embassy. It seems as though some people here feel that Panama and Nicaragua have been saying too many yeses to each other these days, and people are here to protest.

Some day it may be possible to know better how to say yes and no. But in the meantime, if we must err, I hope we can do it on the side of generosity.

ELEVEN

LA VIEJA
The Old Woman

I saw her
in the doorway
of the house
down the road,

an old woman
waiting out
the early morning hours
before the light
of a new day
would give her away.

She hovered
in a corner
not her own
partly covered
by a worn *chamarra*
the color of the wall
she hoped
would hide her.

But I saw her
and wondered
who knew
or has forgotten
to remember her
as she spends the evening
of her night-time
years alone.

There must have been
other times,
a lover
or some children,
her being held gently
or roughly
who can tell
except for
the harsh markings
left on her face
visible
even beneath the blanket
and the meagre
morning light,

markings of age
of tiredness
on her skin,
carved in her heart
as the stigmata
of her years.

And she rose
as did the sun

not to warm
the earth
but to disappear
into the streets
into the morning crowds,
as an old woman
of many
poor and dry
waiting for
another night's corner.

TWELVE

BETHY
Searching for Home

SOMETIMES I hardly know where I am. Or rather, at times I feel so out of place, removed from what I know and love. Often my memory flies back to my country, El Salvador, to days when I was a young girl. I recall the colors and sounds of my childhood, the rich smells of home and of the fields after a rain. I lived in the countryside, up in the mountains. My village in Chalatenango was small but very lovely. It was built in the traditional Spanish style, with a plaza in the middle, planted with trees and flowers, with a lovely garden that old Tió Ernesto kept fresh as spring almost all year round.

My childhood days were happy ones, though I may have edited my memory a bit. The trouble in El Salvador hadn't developed then into the intensity of what it is now: constant violence and a reign of fear. The history of our small country is a sad one. It is a history of poverty for the mass of people, and wealth and power for the few. From time to time the poor would erupt and shout, "No!" And usually they would pay dearly for their shouts. But now again they are refusing merely to eat the crumbs that the *Catorce* — the oligarchy — leave. They are fighting for a better future; they are fighting for justice. But oh, *tanta sangre,* so much blood and suffering. It wasn't that way when I grew up.

As I said, our village was small so I knew almost everyone. Life was lived with bright and primary colors, intense and full of joy, like traditional Salvadoran folk art. My family didn't have much money, but we were not poor. My parents saw that all of their children got a good education. I was even able to attend the Universidad Nacional.

But here I am, far away from my homeland. At times it is unbearable for me. I'm like a woman whose lover has gone far away and whose return is uncertain. A basic part of me is missing.

Most of my family has had to leave the country because of the war. My *marido,* Martín, is an Episcopal priest. He also cannot go back to work in El Salvador. It would be too dangerous for him. He has already lost two brothers in the violence of our country. So here we are — Martín and I — in Panama, a place and culture very different from El Salvador.

True, the people here speak Spanish and the culture is *latino.* But the food, the customs, the music, the architecture, and the way of life are so strange to me, even more painfully strange for the similarities. That is why I like coming up to Monte Claro. The *campesinos* here are a lot like the people I knew in El Salvador: people of the land, weighed down by the heaviness of their history, but with an irrepressible fire remaining in their eyes.

I'm sitting alone in the Casa Comunal in Monte Claro. Ricardo has gone up the hill to find Chan and Flores. We need to talk to them about a work project in the community scheduled for this weekend. The sky has suddenly turned

very dark as it so often does this time of year. I can hear
thunder in the distance, but there is no rain yet. In this calm
before the storm I have a chance to think a bit. And my
mind — no, my heart — has taken me back for a moment
to Chalatenango, El Salvador.

But it is here in Monte Claro where I am for now, and
I need to make the best of it. More than that, I need and
want to be committed to the people of this *aldea*. I have
been working here for over three years, as a social worker for
the Episcopal diocese of Panama. I have come to know this
community, and they have come to know and trust me. That
sort of knowing and trusting doesn't come easily. And this
month marks the completion of two years of work together
here with Padre Ricardo, my *compañero*.

¡Ay, Dios mío! when he first came here I thought "this
will never work!" I have a hard time with *gringos* anyway.
They all seem so arrogant, just like their government. And
when I remember what the *norteamericanos* have done to
my country over the years, I get livid with rage. So can I be
blamed for having a hard time trusting the *gringo*?

Well, I had to work with Ricardo and make the best of it,
¿No? At first I couldn't figure him out. Why was he here? Why
did he want to work among the forgotten people of Monte
Claro when he could have stayed comfortably at the cathedral in the City? He came in the height of the rainy season
when no one in their right mind comes out into the *campo*.
Mud and water are everywhere. It's a real struggle getting
in and out of places like this. Nevertheless he came, week
by week. He didn't seem to mind the mud or the rain. He
would come to visit or to celebrate the Eucharist no matter
what, *no importa el tiempo* — whatever the weather. I was
impressed.

But in those first few months he was a bit pathetic. He had a hard time understanding the accent of the people. And worse, as far as I was concerned, he knew little or nothing about the *campesino* culture. But at least he knew his limitations. He knew he had to do more listening than talking, and so we got along. It was during this time I came to trust him. He was not like the other *gringos* I had known. He knew he didn't have many ready answers to the mountain of problems the poor have in this country. I knew it was hard for him at times, even though he didn't show it much. But I have seen him cry, and so I know.

Ay, there is so much to do here. I have been trying to organize the people to work on a project to bring potable water into the community. Imagine! Here is a community of over 250 people without safe drinking water! The Canadian government has given us a grant to buy materials. But the community needs to plan, organize, and do much of the manual labor. Work goes very slowly here. At times, I know, I get impatient with the community, especially with the men. *Los flojos,* I call them, the weak and ineffectual ones. I speak my mind directly to the people. They understand me, and I understand them. We all know that we care deeply about each other, but someone has to do the shouting and screaming. Ricardo is more — how do you say — gentle. No, "lenient" is better. I think it is partly his personality. But also it is because he is an *extranjero,* a stranger who does not have the same right to criticize in the way that I, a *latina,* a woman of Central America, do. In a way, these are my people! Nevertheless, Ricardo and I complement each other well. Sometimes, though, I wish he would be more authoritative in his approach to the community. The people here respect authority. *¡Caramba!* I never thought I would hear myself say that! Ricardo and I talk together a lot about these things, and that is one reason I have come to enjoy working with him.

The rain has finally come. A real *aguacero,* a cloudburst! The rich smell of decay and fecundity fills the air. At least I'm sitting where I can keep dry. I wonder where Padre, Chan, and Flores are. If we wait too long we won't be able to cross the *quebrada* to return to the City. One time we had to wait four hours for the water to recede before we could cross the stream. That was the time we returned to Sr. Rómulo's *rancho* and had a wonderful time drinking *chicha* and talking. We told stories, laughed, and argued, bathing in the delight of our *convivencia.* I remember that afternoon as one of my happiest ever in Monte Claro.

I almost always love to come here, but especially in May and June when the mangos are ripe. Everyone here knows that Bethy loves mangos, green ones or ripe, it makes no difference. During mango season when I come up the dirt path into the center of Monte Claro the children come running, each trying to be the first to climb a tree and pick a mango for me. I love it. Usually when I leave to return to the City my *chacara* is full of mangoes. At every house where I stop, people give me a mango or two.

Bien pues, life is more than mangos and *convivencia.* Several weeks ago Ricardo and I came to the village to meet with its leaders. We wanted to talk about forming a *comité de emergencia,* an emergency committee to help the community during times of crisis. With the way things are going in the government here, I think we will have enough crises to keep us busy. What I hoped most of all was that the community would organize itself for this support, that it would be able to respond in a prepared way to its own needs. It doesn't always have to be dependent on rescues from the outside.

Well, you would have thought that Padre and I had come to organize a band of *guerrilleros,* guerrilla fighters. *¡Ay, Dios mío!* the people were in an uproar. Mostly they were afraid, I think. Afraid of their future. Afraid of changes they don't understand. Afraid of doing anything but standing still and passively accepting what comes. Our hope had been to do some *concientización* in light of the current reality in Panama and plan for caring for each other when food, medical supplies, or work would not be available. We needed to be prepared to cope when the political situation became more critical or uncertain.

We found the fear to be deeper than we had imagined, especially fear of the political situation. The people felt that what we were trying to do was organize them in opposition to the government, and they were terrified of the consequences of that. Admittedly the analysis we did together led to some strong criticism of the current abuse of power in Panama and of the growing threat of militarism: both Panamanian and that of the United States.

So we had several days of needing to come back to the community and talk with the people, to hear what their concerns were, their misunderstandings of what we had hoped to do. It wasn't all misunderstanding, though. Some of their fear came from hearing each other for the first time give names to their harsh reality. It was as if we needed to hear the bad news before we could begin to hear the good.

We regrouped and decided not to organize a *comité de emergencia,* at least by that name. It is easier, and more acceptable at this point to deal with specific needs, one by one, as they emerge. But we keep talking, keep reflecting together. And I think we are developing more confidence as we do it. We are also becoming clearer that we do not have to struggle alone. The community is finding its faith and solidarity to be its own most trustable resource.

I can laugh about it all now. But then, hardly. Even old Señora Lupita thought that what we were going to do was to arm the people so that they could protect themselves. *¡Qué barbaridad!* I can hardly image her running up and down the hills with a rifle slung over her back.

Martín and I had shown some members of the community a film about Christian base communities in Salvador. In one of the scenes young men and women were at a *misa* out in the countryside, receiving communion with guns slung over their backs. They were members of local defense committees formed to protect villages in areas of conflict. Maybe that's where the idea came from, that we were going to start passing out weapons. Visual images speak more powerfully than words.

All of these *fracasos,* these mistakes we made, are being

turned into something good. The crises have come, especially the food shortages. But we have ways now of working with the community to determine where the needs are and how resources should be shared when we have them. Shortly after the nullified national elections a few weeks ago, several men of the village were being hunted down by government party officials, probably to arrest them. The community rallied to provide protection and help to families who were threatened. It is all so complicated. But I'm glad we had those meetings a few weeks ago, at least to prepare us for what was and is to come.

When I work like this, when I get involved in the lives and struggles of these people, I sometimes become very impatient with the church, with the church as institution, I mean. Maybe its because I'm the wife of a priest that I get so tired of churches. Maybe it's because I work at the diocesan office, and I see the institution from the inside. I tell Ricardo that I don't know whether or not I believe in what the church believes. He listens well, and usually silently. He knows I really do believe in following Jesus, in being a radically committed person, committed to the holy work of liberating and empowering God's people who are oppressed. But I don't always know if that's what the church wants to be doing. Is it really a church for and of the poor? Most of the time I don't think so. At times here in Monte Claro I almost begin to believe it might be true. But I play the agnostic at times, the loyal sceptic to Ricardo's more hopeful heart.

At home I have two daughters: little Lizbeth and her older sister Elizabeth. Elizabeth just celebrated her *quinceaños,* the completion of her first fifteen years, and the celebration of her becoming a woman. How beautiful she was at her fiesta — *¡Tan bonita!* I am very proud of her, but also worried. She has grown up mostly outside of her native El Salvador. She knows very little about it and its way of life. She is very Panamanian, and sadly too much identified with the upper classes here. She goes to a private *colegio,* an Episcopal school in the City where a lot of rich people's children go. She goes not because she is rich, but because she has a scholarship. So I worry about her, worry about what longings and values she will carry into her adult life.

Little Lizbeth, *la gordita,* the chubby one, is almost always with me. She is too young to go to school yet, so I often take her around wherever I go. She likes to come to Monte Claro for they spoil her here. She has many, many *abuelitas* (grandmothers) in Monte Claro.

I can hear Ricardo and the other men coming over the hill now. The rain has stopped, mostly. The *ranas* (frogs) have begun chirping again in the distant mud holes. Coming over the hilly pathways must be almost impossible for the men, with mud as slippery as fresh soap.

Recently the small congregation here was able to raise money to buy a parcel of land not far from the Casa Comunal. We hope to develop it for a cooperative vegetable garden, to help people learn to raise some new kinds of crops to provide extra food for the community. Some of the members of the Junta Misionera also would like to build a cooperative *tienda* there, a small store that would sell basic food supplies, like rice or eggs or flour. It could be run by the community or by people who join the cooperative, with proceeds going back into community projects. At this point there are no *tiendas* in the community. People have to walk a long way to buy a pound of *frijoles.* So this afternoon Chan, Flores, Ricardo, and I will begin to plan for a community meeting to explore some possible uses for this new land

and to think about the suggestion of inviting someone to the community to help us learn about developing a cooperative.

For me this kind of work, working directly with the people, walking with them through their fears and struggles, planning for the future, even when there seems to be no future: these things are what following Jesus is about. The *misas* are good. But they only touch me when they become celebrations of what is real in our actions, celebrations of what we have touched and formed, of what we have learned and begun to change, of the *caminar,* the walking together we do as sisters and brothers, with dignity and courage even in the face of a mountain of opposition. When we do this together we can celebrate the *misa* with integrity, not just as a hollow, merely spiritual thing, something removed from the daily struggles and victories of life. For me that kind of spirituality is pure escape.

I talk a tough line, don't I? One truth is that I really believe in what I have said. The other truth is that I too get afraid and immobilized. I look for my escapes, just like the people I criticize. I'm not as tough as I seem. Ricardo knows that, *gracias a Dios*. And so we have been good companions.

Having companions and being where the important struggles and celebrations of life are experienced and shared: maybe these things will help me find a home. Maybe immersing myself in the reality around me will help me touch again the part within me that has been torn away and misplaced somewhere, now able to be found again. Maybe....

I do know that little by little this community, this place with its scarred hills and hidden ravines, red mud and mango trees: this place is becoming more and more like home to me.

THIRTEEN

CHAN
Compañeros

I HAD better keep working for the day is slipping by quickly. Eliezar is with me. He's the third of my sons, but the oldest left with us now. Eliezar is a part of my second family, my first wife having died more than ten years ago. "Liso," as we call my son, is almost twelve years old now. *¡Caramba!* how fast he has grown. He is strong and quiet like me. But, my God, how he works! He learns quickly all I try to teach him. Some day he will be caring for Mari and me. I have to teach him well.

I remember the time he first used a *machete*. He was about five years old and had come out into the field to be with me. I left him for a moment to go down to the stream to get some water to drink, and when I returned, there he was with my *machete,* chopping down corn stalks, one by one. I tried to pretend I was angry. "The *machete* is dangerous, Liso, and you are too young. Beside the corn isn't ripe yet." I scolded but without much conviction; and by his smile I knew he understood. I was proud. My son will be a boy one day, then a man. But I still have a lot to teach him.

I was proud because of what the *machete* symbolizes for us in the *campo*. It speaks of courage, of strength, and of skill. A good *machetero* can do almost anything with his *machete*. It is a sign that one is a man. So little Liso felt like a man that day, just like his Papa. How could I be mad at him? We men have a saying in our village: *"Para mí sólo el machete y mis compañeros; es mi vida.* For me there is only my *machete* and my companions; these are my life." Life is more than these things, ¿*No?* And certainly the *machete* can be a sign of the uglier sides of *machismo.* But for a moment I saw my little son strong and tall, about to become a man.

Well, the May sun is hot and I've only a little time left to plant my seeds for the coming growing season. In spite of the heat the rains have just begun, and the Feast of San Isidro Labrador, St. Isidore the Worker, is about here. This year the fiesta will be special, for we have named our new chapel La Iglesia San Isidro Labrador. I think it is the only Episcopal Church in the world with that name. According to our Latin American tradition all the planting has to be done by May 15, the day of San Isidro, so that the harvest will be plentiful.

As I look out over my field I can see in the distance the newly finished chapel. It is lovely, painted blue and white against the dark green hills. It is our church, we helped build it, and we in the community are very proud of it. I am especially proud because it was my idea that we name it after San Isidro. Let me tell you how that came about.

Several months ago Padre Ricardo told us that it was time to think about naming the chapel. He wanted the community to consider some names and to talk about them together. Once we had chosen one or two names, we would submit them to the bishop for his approval. We had never named a church before! *¡Ay, Dios mío,* what an opportunity!

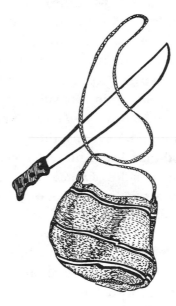

*"A good machetero can do almost anything
with his machete . . .*

Padre shared with us that in the Anglican tradition
churches were named after saints as a way of remembering the church's story, of remembering men and women
who were "lights in their several generations," he said, people whose lives and witness were important for the memory
and mission of the church. Also, he said, naming a church
can say to us and to others what is important to us, how
we want to be known. The *santo patronal*, the patron saint
of a church, shows something of what the community feels
about its mission. So we all began to think.

Every one here has his or her favorite saint, the saint
who has been helpful in difficult spots from time to time.
So we all began to suggest our favorites. Santiago, Santa

María, San José, San Francisco, and San Marcos were frequently mentioned. Each one of these saints is popular in Panama, especially among *campesinos*. I suggested San Isidro because he was a poor man like us and because he has traditionally been the patron saint of *campesinos*. He too was a farmer. Many people thought my idea was a good one. I smiled quietly to myself, but tried not to show my enthusiasm. The people together will need to decide.

For several weeks we talked about this naming. Years ago, when the English first planted Anglican churches in Central America, they brought over names of saints that meant something to them, names that were a part of their heritage. But we wanted a name that came from our history, that reflected something of our story and traditions. Some people, I knew, wanted to choose this or that saint because its festival would be very popular and a lot of money could be made by pilgrims who would come from other villages to the *fiesta*. Others had beliefs about the power of this or that saint, *palanca* we call it here, a special influence with God. But Padre tried to help us be clear about why we choose a name, and what this name would mean as we tried to live together as a Christian people, serving God and serving our community.

After almost three months we had agreed on a name to give to the bishop: San Isidro Labrador. We waited anxiously to see if the bishop would go along with our choice. After all it was something new for the Episcopal Church. But it was a name that we could identify with very deeply. At last, *gloria a Dios,* came the answer, Yes!

The next Sunday during the *misa* we talked about our new name and what it could mean for us. We talked about how San Isidro could help us to remember the dignity of

our work. How this name could remind us of the importance of compassion, generosity, and mutual respect. Isidro,
who lived in Madrid, Spain, in the twelfth century, had great
concern for his poor community. Though he had only little
himself, he always shared what he had. He always helped
his *compañeros* to work hard on the land and to treat God's
earth with respect, as *tierra sagrada,* sacred earth. Naming
our church San Isidro Labrador also helps us to remember
that we who are humble and poor as was Isidro have value
to each other and before God.

I have been thinking about San Isidro lately, thinking how
for me it is easier to believe in a good man like Isidro than it
is to believe in God. I keep these thoughts mostly to myself.
They are probably foolish. But for me they are real. For years
it has been hard for me to believe in God. What God do
I believe in? The angry God who punishes us when we do
wrong, the God I grew up knowing? Or the God who loves
and cares, the God Padre Ricardo talks so much about? Most
of the time I just give up; I can't even picture God in my
head. Yet I still believe, but not in someone I can't figure
out or imagine.

Besides I have always had a hard time trusting in God
because my life has been so hard. I have prayed a lot to God,
asking God to help me or my family. I prayed for God to heal
my first wife, and she died. I pray to God to help me not be
so poor, and I'm still poor. I pray to God to help my children
not be sick, and they still get sick. We almost lost little Lupita
several months ago. *¡Ay, Dios mío!* I pray and try to believe,
but nothing changes.

I try to picture Jesus instead of God. Jesus was a person
like I am. But even here it's hard for me, for Jesus suffered
too much. I know that a lot of our religion in Panama focuses

on the Jesus of the Cross. But I have problems with that; I don't think that people should suffer. Nor do I believe that suffering is needed to become good. If that were true, all of us *carajos,* rascals, here in Monte Claro would be as pure as angels. We certainly have suffered enough. So even thinking of Jesus doesn't always help me. I need something more concrete, more flesh and blood, something more "here."

What helps me more than anything in life are my *compañeros,* those who walk with me, care for me, and let me care for them. For us *latinos* the word *compañero,* companion, is a very beautiful word. A *compañero* is someone who eats *pan* (bread) with you, someone who shares your life, who accompanies you even when life is painful and full of tears. I have friends like that. And I am beginning to believe that the church in Monte Claro will be a *compañero.* Padre and Bethy are *compañeros.* So are my friends Flores and Catalino and Agustín. So is my wife, Mari. Even though it's hard for me, I keep believing in God, and I keep believing because of these companions in my life, because of real people like San Isidro who have lived with compassion and helped us live with joy.

Well, as I said, I keep these ideas to myself most of the time. I don't think that many people would accept me with these thoughts, unless, of course, they too have the same thoughts. How can I know? I think that Padre would not judge me. He has said things at the *misa* that make me believe he would understand. But I don't know for sure. So I keep quiet.

All of this thinking reminds me of how important *compañeros* are. Alone we are nothing. Together, *juntos,* we can be full, especially of hope. I remember a day several months ago. It was still the summer in Panama, that is, the dry season. The people of Monte Claro organized a bus trip to visit the family of Ismael Santana, the senior warden of the church here. His family lives where many of us came from, in the province of Coclé about three hours from here.

We got up early that Saturday morning, all of us who could go, and arrived in Quebrada Ancha just before noon. It was up in the mountains where the air was cool and clear, real *campo*. Many family members and friends were there to greet us. It was a day of great celebration. Padre was with us too, along with Padre Martín, Bethy's husband, to celebrate the Eucharist out in the *patio*.

What I remember most was our return. We had ridden in the bus for about a half an hour after leaving Ismael's family and came to a *quebrada*, a ravine filled with flowing water. Someone suggested we stop to see the *cascada*, the waterfall below. So we all got out of the bus and climbed down the ravine. It was too much, too tempting. Before long everyone was in the water, swimming and playing like we had never done since we were children. Even Padre and Bethy were playing like ducks, with delightful abandon. The sky was clear and warm. There was no sound of cars or trucks. There was only the wind and the whistle of birds overhead. This is what I mean by saying that life only matters with *compañeros*, with people who will go with you, to play or to cry. That day we played, more than I remember having done for years.

As I said, Mari too is my *compañera*. She has been a steady friend and wife for fifteen long years. Life has been hard for us. And sometimes I have been hard on her. But we are *compañeros*.

We don't get to play much. But I remember many times making *tamales* with her before Christmas, *tamales* we sell in the community or in town. It is almost like play. Together we soak the dry kernels of corn and later grind them into mush. Then we cook the chicken we will use and stew some fruit if we have it. Together we walk to the stream to collect leaves for wrapping the *tamales*. And together we shape the corn meal around small pieces of chicken and fruit, wrapping each one in the leaves and throwing them into the *paila* of boiling water on the *fogón,* the wood fire. And all the while we talk. We remember things we've shared and watch our children running all over the patio, dirty for the mud, but happy. We remember how God has blessed us with so many children, and with *compañeros* and *compañeras.* We don't play together often. But making *tamales* each December is close to play.

We so often say to each other, *"Qué Dios te acompañe,"* "May God go with you." Maybe I'm not so crazy in my head for thinking that *compañeros,* people who accompany us, help us to believe in God. *Bien pues,* it's how I feel. And having little Liso with me in the field today makes me very happy inside me.

We have a lot left to do before the Feast of San Isidro. This year I'm going to plant more. In the community we are worried about the economic situation in Panama, concerned about how it is getting worse. So we had better be prepared. It means a lot more work this year, preparing the fields, with energy we hardly have. But we are all planting more.

I'm planting *maíz,* as usual. Along with the corn I'll plant *yuca,* a sweet root we always eat. I also grow *guandu,* a wonderfully flavored pea we use with rice. I plant rice too, and *frijoles.* And always there are *plátanos* on my *finca,* my little plot of land.

When it rains on the Feast of San Isidro, it is a good sign. It hasn't rained much yet this season, *gracias a Dios*. But after the planting we'll need a lot of rain. May God remember us here in Monte Claro. May San Isidro bless our fields and our planting. We are very poor here. But I do not believe our poverty is a disgrace. Nor does it automatically make us good. It is just the way it has always been for us. But the more I think of it, the more I realize we are rich in *compañeros*.

"*Oy, Liso,*" I call to my son. "*Ven conmigo, vamos a regresar,* Let's go back now." My little *compañero* — I let him carry my *machete* back to the house.

FOURTEEN

DON TINO
El Sombrero

THERE are about fifteen regional styles of hats in my country, Panama. Such a small country and so many *sombreros, ¿No?* Well, it's a very hot country, with sun and rain pounding down on us continually. We may not need much clothing, but we need our hats. *La necesidad hace maestro;* necessity is the mother of invention. Out of the need to survive in this furnace of a country we have turned hat making into an art.

I remember watching my mother weave hats in the afternoon, when her daily chores were completed. We lived up in the mountains of Coclé, and my father and mother knew all the traditional arts of that area. My mother would weave hats almost every day, sitting with other women and sharing the local gossip. My mother told me that she had learned to make hats just before she married my father. Two hats were to be her first gift to him as her husband: one hat for work in the fields and one for dress.

My wife weaves too. At the beginning of each rainy season she collects the hearts of palm, strips them, making long

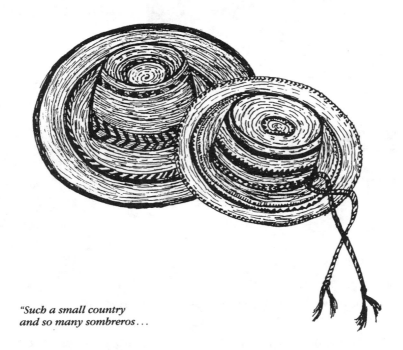

*"Such a small country
and so many sombreros...*

strands of material to weave, and sets them out to dry. Some
are dyed black or brown to use for artistic designs in her
hats. I miss seeing her weave silently each day. When she was
younger she used to sell her hats; but later she made them
only for family or friends. She is a wonderful hat maker. But
now she is gone.

With my fifty-five years I feel old, and so often tired. People in Monte Claro look to me too much for advice or to
solve problems. I would just like to be left alone most of the
time — to make hats, perhaps. But somehow I can't let go.
I can't stop being who I am, and for years now I have been
the *jefe*, the chief of this poor village. I can't even remember
how I got chosen. I just was, and now I can't shake it.

The *señora*, my wife, has gone. For a long time — as
long as I can remember — she has been suffering from some

problem in her mind. She often told people that someone had put a curse on her. It's possible, I guess. But I don't believe that's the problem. For days at a time she would withdraw in silence. Then, sometimes, she would shout and make everyone's life hard for days. When she was like this I would think of not coming home. But the children needed me. And so did she.

Sometimes she would run away, usually to some of her family in Coclé. She would be gone for several weeks. But always she would come back, bringing the new hats she had made. And things would be calm for a long while. Now she has gone, and this time it feels like forever. I miss her. But life has been calmer. Only my daughter and her child are with me. Sarai, my daughter, is very good to me. She cooks and cleans the house, and cares for the animals when I am not around. She knows I am sad, though she doesn't talk about it. But somehow her knowing makes it easier.

A few weeks ago I gave Padre Ricardo a new hat, a *sombrero cocléño* — a hat in the style of the men of the province of Coclé. It had a feather from a wild pheasant and a colorful woven band around it. I wish that Mariela, my wife, could have made it. It was a gift to Padre for his *despedida,* his farewell. After three years of working among us he will be returning to the United States. I hope the hat will help him not to forget us. We are the people of hats, true?

As I tell some of my story, I guess I am still sad for Padre's departure. There is more than enough sadness in my life to tell. But right now my grief is for losing a good friend. When Padre and Bethy were here I had begun to hope again. We dreamed and planned and saw changes happen. They were good years. I wonder if we can keep up the dreaming. Ricardo said that holy seeds had been planted among us, seeds that did not depend on him or on me alone. The people here are different now. We know how to do things we never knew before. And we are more of a community, more of a people who will keep struggling together for a better life. Sometimes I am able to believe this.

I remember how hopeful I felt, even within my sadness, when I sang at Padre's *despedida* — his farewell. When I was young my father taught me to sing the *saloma,* the traditional, improvised songs or chants of the countryside. We would sing at work in the fields. We would sing for fiestas. We would sing, sometimes, for the death of one we loved. My father was proud of me. I was one of the most loved *salomeros* of the region.

But that was long ago. I hadn't sung for years, and there I was singing at the *misa* for Ricardo's departure. I sang to invite the people to prayer. I sang to remind us all of what had happened during the past four years or so. I sang to honor Padre. I sang to express the grief of us all.

The *salomas* are a remarkable kind of expression. At times for me they seem like a soulful, even drunken cry of sorrow. At other times they express a passionate joy. I remember my father singing in the fields. At times an answer would come across the hills; completely by surprise it would come. Someone else was working alone and heard the greeting sung across the distance, breaking the early morning silence. There was a kind of communion, a celebration from afar between two strangers or, perhaps, friends.

As a surprise, I had invited some old friends from Antón, a town near the province where I was born. I invited them to come down to Monte Claro to play their music. Old Tito brought his *tambor,* his drum. Fidel brought his fiddle with only three strings. And Pepito brought his *concertina.* It took them a whole day to get to Monte Claro, so they stayed overnight at my house. During the *misa* they played some of our traditional songs. Later they played while the men danced to the *montañeros,* the mountain songs of our past. Everyone brought festival hats: *sombreros* from Los Santos, Coclé, and Herrera. Our dances and hats go together. Hats that cover speak of the hidden side of our culture. Songs and dances, more transparent, let others into the heart of our people, into lives and culture that are not easily shared. So I guess we need both our *sombreros* and our *salomas.*

When I sang that day I was as proud and happy as I was sad. I was proud for who we were as a community, for our culture and traditions. For our faith that gathered us that day around the altar. For all of the things we had accomplished during three or four years. For the small seeds of hope sown among us. But I wept for losing a friend. And, perhaps I wept for fear, for not knowing what will happen to us now. For all this I sang.

A few days later, a day or two before Padre was to leave Panama, he came to my house with Padre Julio, his new assistant. I had invited them for lunch, so that we could spend one last time together. Sarai and I had made some *sancocho,* the best we could make. I am known in the community for being a good cook. So we had a real fiesta together — Padre, Julio, Sarai, and I. The day was clear, without rain. There was a slight breeze coming over the hills. A rare Monte Claro day. We sat and talked for several hours. We did some remembering. Some laughing at mistakes we'd made. Some acknowledging of how far we'd come together as a community. We talked about the troubles of our small country. I felt as though we were sharing together as brothers.

Padre wore his new hat. He asked me if the *señora* had

made it. He had often watched her make hats, and had wanted her to make one for him some day, but was too shy to ask.

I remembered the first time he had come to my house. He was new in the community, and I had asked him to come to visit and to bless our home. My wife had been causing trouble for several days before, going through one of her "spells." She really confused Padre. He couldn't figure her out. Was she crazy, or was he? He didn't seem to know. There he was blessing the house after his visit, with Mariela shouting something incomprehensible, and a couple of roosters pecking at his ankles for having invaded their territory. He tried not to notice. And I tried not to laugh. It was as comical as it was painful for me. *¡Ay, Dios!* Somehow we get through it all.

My house sits on the top of a hill, the highest one in the community. It has been well cared for during the twenty years I have been here. I have coffee bushes, fruit trees of all kinds, and a collection of animals — some for eating, some for selling, some as friends. *¡Basta ya!* It is like a zoo here at times. Our house and *patio* show that a lot of love has been given to it. Mariela, when she is well, does a lot to keep things looking beautiful, especially in the garden. When I have time and when I am not too tired from my work, I too like to work around the *patio,* cleaning and planting and rebuilding. From the edge of our *patio* we can see almost all of the village.

I can see the *ranchito* of my neighbors, Mili and Roberto. So young, these two. But having lived so richly, so painfully their few years. Looking down on their house makes me remember the Christmas child. Not too long ago they had a child, a beautiful boy blessed with big eyes and long, dark hair. Mili was only sixteen when she had her child. Roberto, twenty. Both sets of parents forbade the marriage. But the two young ones married anyway. So they were alone, except for some cousins who took pity on them and took them under the wing.

Mili and Roberto were filled with delight when they were asked to offer their newborn boy for the Christmas pageant in Monte Claro. It was the first pageant ever for our community, and their *varoncito* was to be the child Jesus. The pageant was wonderful, if a bit chaotic, with many children taking part in their usual improvised way. Mari read the story from the Bible, and the children, dressed in costumes, played the parts. The baby smiled silently all through the reading.

You can hardly imagine the surprise and grief the young couple felt when the child died a few days later. No one knows yet why he died. He was rushed to the children's hospital in the City one night, and never lived to see the morning. Padre helped Mili and Roberto bury the child. Because the child hadn't yet been registered, the parents had a very hard time claiming the body. Like Joseph centuries ago, they had no proof that they were the parents. *¡Qué triste!*

For a while people in the community were afraid. Why would God let a child die who had been the baby Jesus in the pageant? Many people said that perhaps we should not do that anymore, have a live baby to be the child Jesus. I think that the people were simply shocked and surprised that a child who was enjoyed so much by the community one day in a few days would be gone. It didn't make sense. *No todo el monte es orégano*, we say. Things aren't always as we would want them. But the memory remains a very hard one, especially for Roberto and Mili. *¡Ay, Dios!* life is so uncertain.

In spite of the uncertainty of our future in Monte Claro, I'm feeling more and more able to be the kind of leader I want to be. Bethy and Padre have helped me to trust my abilities. Sometimes it is easier for outsiders to help you see yourself in new ways. Those closest to me, my family or community, can't often help with that. But Padre and Bethy really listened. They paid attention to what I told them. Followed advice I gave them. They seem to honor who I am, what I can offer to this community.

I used to try to fix everything, to mediate every conflict, to smooth over every hard feeling. Now I know I can't do that. Everyone must take his or her own responsibility for problems in the community. As we say here sometimes, *"Cada uno sabe donde le aprieta el zapato."* "We all know where our own shoe pinches."

I'm more *suave* now in how I lead my people. I don't try to dominate as much any more. I try rather to be an example. I try to be a person of vision and of hope. I try to work with others. It's better that way.

I only hope that I don't get lost in my sadness. Like my wife, I want to withdraw when I become sad. I don't want to be with people, to work with them, to dream with them. But more and more I know that when I feel lost, when I feel I want to run away, that's when I need to find my friends and be with them. That's what I did when I invited Padre and Julio, the new deacon working among us, to come for *sancocho*. Padre, my friend, when he came up the hill that day with his new *sombrero* pushed way back on his head like the men from Coclé wear them, coming up the hill smiling as if he were a *campesino, un poco borracho,* a bit tipsy. I knew somehow I would be all right. I had chosen to deal with my sadness by inviting friends over to be with me. I had decided to live and act as if I weren't alone.

A few months ago, before Padre left, the community organized its first *junta local,* its first town committee, recognized by the *junta local* of Arraiján. I was chosen as the first *alcalde,* the first mayor. I felt very honored. Probably a year or so ago I wouldn't have felt that way. I remember coming to the first meeting of the *junta,* dressed as well as I could be, wearing my brown leather hat, my finest. I must have been a sight. But I dressed the way I felt. I was mayor of a real community, respected by most everyone. Ha! It's amazing what a good hat will do for me!

Well, enough! I can't sit here all day, hat in hand waiting. Yes, I miss Ricardo. I miss the years we had, with all their frustrations as well as their times of joy. I miss a lot more than I can give words to. But it's interesting to me: here we are, all of us Panamanians, with our poor country coming apart for all its struggles, and Monte Claro is daring to look toward the future. We've come so far. We have so many plans. Now we are more a people of hope than of despair. God is good. And our poor life is good, even with all the tears. I think we just weave these tears into our joy and our struggles, weave them like new and cherished patterns of our *sombreros,* and get on with things.

I only hope my *señora,* Mariela, will return one day to share this life with me.

CAMINANDO
Journeying

F OR me the stories I have shared speak of a journey. It was a short journey, at least for me, of a mere three years. But all journeys have a beginning, and it has been mostly of this that I have written. The continuance will be with others, with those who will pick up the loose threads of what has begun, weaving them with both continuity and change.

The people who have spoken in these stories continue on together as they always have, but with a difference. What has been shared in these stories, at least as far as I can see, is a truth that has emerged from a kind of beginning. Something new has happened. Something fresh was sown among the people of Monte Claro. For a time strangers walked with them. We walked in ways that challenged, in ways that encouraged, and in ways that sought to discover and draw out a long, dormant hope.

The strangers were a North American priest and a Salvadoran woman, along with other *compañeros* from time to time from the Episcopal diocese of Panama. These companions — at least Ricardo and Bethy — were changed as much

136

as were those they came to be among for a while. These stories, even as they are retold in the reading, continue the change, continue to affect those who remember and those who hear for the first time. For this reason stories are told — that the memory of a people might not be lost and in the remembering people near and distant might be touched by the grace of life lived deeply and with commitment in struggle and hope.

Dom Helder Camara, archbishop of Recife, Brazil, passionate advocate of the poor, advocate of the voiceless whose stories have not yet been remembered, let alone told — Dom Helder once said:

No people are so poor that they cannot give;
likewise, none are so rich that they cannot receive.

The stories of the people are rich in their giving. They are rich in the way they tell the truth, mostly without bitterness or despair. There is much sadness in the lives and stories of the people of Monte Claro, but it is a sadness spoken with hope, shared with a kind of undefeated spontaneity and joy. True, in Monte Claro there is at times a caution bordering on fatalism. Promises and hopes brought in from the outside do not play well among the people of this community. Any hope, any promise able to survive has to come from within them. And the sowing and birthing of this kind of hope is slow and tentative business. The struggle and tears of generations will not be wiped away easily.

As the people of Monte Claro were encouraged to tell their stories — something that happened little by little over a period of more than three years — something new started to happen. In the living and struggling and in the reflecting together on their life, a new capacity to see and hold together contradictory things began to be possible. Along with the harshness of life, new expression was given to gentleness. Amid isolation came a growing sense of solidarity. Along with the history of powerlessness came a trust in abilities and gifts. Along with the bitter memories of abandonment began to emerge a new sense of companionship.

These contrasts between many forms of suffering and hope are given expression all through the preceding stories, causing one to wonder, perhaps, how such contradictions can be endured without being resolved either in despair or false hope.

These words are in effect love stories. Like most stories emerging from a love that tries to speak the truth, they are bittersweet. Grace is bittersweet. It leads to a vision that describes the wounds before imagining the healing. It speaks of the bad news that must be faced before the Good News can be "good." And so as the contradictions were faced, so too did a community begin to emerge in which the *caminar* — the journeying — could be possible. Contradictions could be endured if there were a sense of movement, a sense of journey or of a coming-to-be what the God of the journey was creating.

Here is where, I think, the people of Monte Claro, poor and empty though they seem to be, have something rich to offer. They are uneven and fragile people just like you and me. But most of them are people who have begun to challenge the dearest assumptions of their memory and tradition: that nothing can change and that God or fate has determined that their lot is simply to endure patiently the oppressions that are the lot of people of the underside of life. The message within them had been "surrender now, and hope for something better in the next life." But in the place of this traditional attitude of surrender faint cries of protest are beginning to be heard. They are heard in the ever-present songs. They are heard in the small beginnings of community organization, in small projects begun and realized. They are heard through the reflections and prayers of the community's liturgical gatherings.

Within these stories a common vocabulary emerges, words that tremble before new beginnings. These are words that protest the way things have been and that dream about what might yet be. They are words of faith, as well as of a people beginning to feel that God is the God of their day-by-day life and of their future. They are words like solidarity and companionship, mutuality and community, awareness and enablement.

"Cuando el pobre cree en el pobre . . . when the poor begin to believe in themselves . . . " says the song — when what has been seen as humiliating becomes a source of dignity, when dependency grows into self-sufficiency, when weakness becomes empowerment, when failure and self-hate turn into cherishing, when individualism and isolation emerge into community, when sadness is wrapped in beauty — then a people know that the Good News is being proclaimed and lived out among them.

We Christians in the northern and more developed places of the world may not struggle with the crushing oppressions of the historic poor of Latin America. But we are people like them who need to know that the Spirit of God is among us, a Spirit proclaiming good and liberating news. Often our oppressions are less evident to us or are more covered by the busyness and wealth with which we distract ourselves. But we too fear the future. We feel lonely and abandoned. More and more we sense our powerlessness before organizations or forces that determine our future. Militarism, racism, and a rotting environment seem beyond our capacity to understand or redeem. Economic disparity among our people, along with rapid changes in social and family life, often make us throw up our hands with helplessness. Our wealth of education, technology, and choices seem to bury us year by year under mountains of what we neither can understand nor control.

We, like the people of Monte Claro, need someone to help us tell our story, to walk with us faithfully and with hope. We need someone to help us name and bear the contradictions of our life, to help us celebrate and dream, struggle and weep.

The stories we have shared here, if they say anything to us, say that the good and liberating news that Jesus brings among us is the news that we already have what we long for; we already have among us and within us gifts and courage from God, resources enough for healing and renewing. It's not "out there" or "in the future" that we will find hope. Rather, the Kingdom of God is among us like a grain of salt, like a mustard seed, like a small child, or like the first steps of a journey. The Kingdom of God is among us, too, in the lives shared and the stories told by a small community somewhere outside Panama City. Those who are poor have given. And the giving has been rich in truth and in grace.

GLOSSARY

abrazo: hug

aguacero: downpour

alcalde: mayor

aldea: a small hamlet

alma: soul

antillanos: people of West Indian heritage

¡Aquí, regular!: response to "How are you?," meaning "same as usual."

así es la vida: such is life

Balboa: name of Panamanian currency (one Balboa=one dollar)

barrio: a district or neighborhood

¡Basta, ya!: Enough!

bendición: blessing

bien pues: well, then

bonita/o: beautiful; **muy bonita/o:** very beautiful

borracho: drunk

buenos días: good day; **buenas tardes:** good afternoon; **buenas noches:** good night

burrito: little burro

caminar: to walk

campesino: a farmer, rural peasant

campo: countryside

cantina: a local bar

capacitación: enablement, training

carajo: rascal

¡caramba!: exclamation of surprise or annoyance; gracious, darn it!

casa: house

casa comunal: community hall

catorce: fourteen; sometimes, in El Salvador, referring to the oligarchy, the fourteen families who run everything

centavo: penny

chacara: typical Panamanian woven purse

chamarra: shawl, poncho

chancho: dirty one (i.e., pig)

chicha: a drink, usually of fruit juice (in some areas, an alcoholic drink)

chichemi: a popular drink made of corn or rice, with milk and sugar, sometimes spiced

141

chiva: small buses for public transportation

Chocho: name of Pacífico's dog: probably from the verb *chochear*, to act senilely

¡chuleta!: a popular Panamanian exclamation; literally means "pork chop"; expresses surprise, glee, or, at times, frustration

comadre: godmother, or sometimes "midwife"

compadre: godfather, or sometimes a close pal

¿Cómo está(s)?: How are you?

compañero: companion, comrade in the cause

compañera: (feminine)

concientización: consciousness raising, awareness that leads to action

con mucho gusto: with much pleasure

convivencia: fellowship

corazón sagrado de Jesús: Sacred Heart of Jesus

cuento: story

culantro: leafy cousin to coriander, used often in soups, with a strong smell and flavor, basic to Panamanian cooking

cura: name for a priest, curate

curandero: traditional healer

despedida: a farewell

dibujo: pattern, design

Dios mediante: God willing

¡Dios mío!: My God!

egoismo: individualism, negative sense of that term

enamorado/a: man/woman in love

esperanza: hope

extranjero: stranger, foreigner

familiares: extended family

fiesta: party, festival

finca: farm, plot of farming land

finqueros: owners of the fincas

flojo: weak, ineffectual

fogón: simple wood stove

fracaso: mistake, failure

frijoles: beans

gordito: little fat one

gracias a Dios: thanks be to God

gringo: North American (usually not used derisively in Panama)

guandu: a small pea-like vegetable, used with rice

guardia (nacional): (National) police

guayabera: tropical shirt for men

guerrilleros: guerrilla fighters

hermano/a: brother/ sister

hijo: son

huipo: tropical tree with large canopy of leaves

individualismo: individualism

jefe: chief, boss

junta: committee, board

junta comunal: local committee

junta misionera: mission committee

junta parroquial: vestry

juntos: together

ladrones: bandits

latino: a Latin American

lucha: struggle, fight

machete: a long field knife, for cutting grass, cane, etc.

machetero: one who wields a machete

machismo: the flaunting of manliness

maíz: corn

marginados: marginal people

marido: husband

misa: Mass, Holy Eucharist

muñeco: doll

mutualidad: mutuality

novela: TV soap operas

Padre: father, used of priests

padrecito: affectionate name for a priest

padrino: godfather; **madrina:** godmother

paila: large iron pot for cooking

palanca: leverage, influence, clout

paloma: dove

pan: bread

patio: yard

patrón: patron, employer, boss

peón: laborer (usually unskilled)

pesado: heavy, oppressive

plátano: a banana-like tropical fruit, often served fried

plaza: town square

poco a poco: little by little

pollos de patio: yard chickens

primo: cousin

Puente de las Américas: the bridge in Panama City crossing the canal at its opening

puesta del sol: sunset

quebrada: a ravine, a drainage ditch for rain runoff

¡Qué barbaridad!: What rashness!

¡Qué lástima!: What a pity!

¡Qué le vaya bien!: a departing greeting, "May it go well with you"

quinceaños: fifteenth birthday (especially for a girl)

rana: frog

rancho: a small house, made of bamboo and palm

sabor: flavor

sabroso: flavorful, wonderful

saloma: a traditional Panamanian improvised song

salomero: one who sings salomas

sancocho: a favorite Panamanian chicken soup, specially spiced

saril: drink made from the buds of the saril bush, red in color and flavored with ginger; the seeds are used to make a coffee substitute

seco: literally "dry," but used here means a local alcoholic (distilled) beverage made of sugar cane

señor/a: mister, madame (La Señora is usually the wife)

sereno: afternoon breeze

si Dios quiere: God willing

sobrino/a: nephew, niece

solidaridad: solidarity

sombrero: hat

sombrero santeño: hat made in the province of Los Santos

suave: smooth, mild, or gentle

taborete: small portable stool for sitting

tambor: drum

techo de paja: a palm-branch thatched roof for a *rancho*

tienda: a small store

tigre: tiger or any wild cat

tío: uncle

triste: sad; **un poco triste:** a little sad

urbano: city person

varón: male

varoncito: a small boy

¿Verdad?: True? Isn't that so?

viacrucis: way, or stations, of the cross

vieja: old woman

yame: a tropical root, like a sweet potato

yuca: a potato-like root, eaten boiled or fried